Dear

Its hard

to express my affection for you and to say how I respect your work — The students that I have come in contact with (from clague) all stand beside me in saying

You're the best.

Love

[redacted].

ART NOUVEAU

ART NOUVEAU

MALCOLM HASLAM

Macdonald Orbis

A *Macdonald Orbis* BOOK

First published in Great Britain in 1988
by Macdonald & Co (Publishers) Ltd
London & Sydney

A member of BPCC plc

British Library Cataloguing in Publication Data

Haslam, Malcolm
Art nouveau. – (Collectors' style guides).
1. Art objects – Collectors and collecting
2. Art, nouveau
I. Title II. Series
709'.03'49 NK775.5.A7

ISBN 0-356-14542-5

Editor Elizabeth Eyres **Art Editor** Clive Hayball **Picture Research** Elizabeth Loving **Photography** Susanna Price **Designer** Karen Bowen **Filmset** Tradespools Ltd **Printed and bound in Italy** at New Interlitho S.P.A.

Macdonald & Co (Publishers) Ltd
Greater London House
Hampstead Road
London NW1 7QX

ACKNOWLEDGEMENTS

I would like to thank the following for their advice and assistance in the preparation of this book: K. Barlow Ltd., the Furniture Store, John Jesse & Irina Laski Ltd., the Pruskin Gallery, the Purple Shop, Sotheby's, Christie's, Bonham's, Phillips, and all the stallholders at Antiquarius Antiques Market who allowed us to photograph objects from their stock. I am particularly grateful to Margaret Knight of the Victoria & Albert Museum who has contributed the chapters on Furniture and Textiles, Metalwork, Jewellery, and Prints and Posters.

Malcolm Haslam

Picture credits for the Introduction

Architectural Association 14; BBC Hulton Picture Library 11 (top), 13, 17; Louvre, Paris, 10; Musée des Arts Decoratifs 11 (bottom); Musée Carnavalet, Paris/Giraudon 18; Mansell Collection 8, 9, 12, 19; Tate Gallery, London, 15; Victoria & Albert Museum, London, 6.

Author's note on the Price Lists

The price lists are based on auction prices recorded during the last two years in European and American salerooms. For the purposes of the list £1 = $1.60.

The price band given is only a guide. If an item is found which is priced below the lower price given, collectors should make sure that it is genuine, and not damaged or restored. If, on the other hand, the price being asked is higher than the top price given in the list, collectors should ask themselves if the object is of particularly fine quality, particularly large of its sort, very rare, or has some other exceptional feature.

The figure indicating quality of design and/or decoration is largely subjective, and the collector will no doubt find it entertaining to compare his/her own taste with the author's.

CONTENTS

INTRODUCTION

Watercolour design for a printed textile by Charles Rennie Mackintosh, an example of the more geometrical Art Nouveau favoured in Glasgow and Vienna.

'Crumble away, society!' This was the cry of Des Esseintes, the hero of J.K. Huysmans' novel *A Rebours* (Against Nature) published in 1884, who had grown weary in his pursuit of pleasure and was fading away in sheer ennui. All the elaborate diversions which he had devised to sustain himself in an ugly, modern world had failed. In his despair, he uttered the plea of the anarchist.

Eleven years later Henry van de Velde, a Belgian architect and designer, and a pioneer of Art Nouveau, wrote: 'Art is beginning anew because society is beginning anew.' To most of those who created Art Nouveau, and to many of those who consumed its products, the style represented if not a revolt then at least a protest against established values. Towards the end of the nineteenth century, old morals, old laws and old institutions were under attack from a handful of visionaries, socialists, sceptics, writers and artists. *The New Spirit* was the title of a book of essays by the English critic Havelock Ellis, published in 1890, in which he reviewed the progress of the literary and philosophical assault on the old culture. The emphasis on 'New' reflected the impact of the theory of evolution expounded by Charles Darwin and supported by anyone who claimed to hold advanced opinions. It became important to be an originator not an imitator, an individual not one of the crowd.

CREATING A NEW ART

The name 'Art Nouveau' was an expression of the need felt by some artists to lead humanity to a new artistic Utopia where architects and designers would no longer copy old styles, but would instead create an ever original art. They were less aware of the contradiction inherent in their dream than the restraint imposed on them by the existing institutions of the artistic establishment. In most European countries all matters artistic were run by some sort of academy which represented the official taste of the royal court or the republican state. The styles favoured were those of classical antiquity and the Renaissance, which had over the centuries acquired an artistic authority matching their order and clarity, qualities which rulers generally find agreeable.

In Paris, Emperor Napoleon III permitted artists whose works had been excluded from the official Salon of 1863 to show them in public at a Salon des Refusés. Edouard Manet exhibited *Déjeuner sur l'herbe* which showed a party of two men and two women having a meal and a chat beside a river. But the women were *déshabillées*; citizens and Emperor were disgusted. The experiment of the Salon des Refusés was never repeated. The female nude, asserted the guardians of public morals, was acceptable in a classical, historical or religious setting, but not as a human being alive today. The Royal Academician J.C. Horsley, addressing the Church Congress in 1885, had less liberal notions: 'Is not clothedness a distinct type and feature of our Christian faith? All art representations of nakedness are out of harmony with it.' Such an opinion invited ridicule; Oscar Wilde, for one, jeered. He described the presence at one of Lady Windermere's receptions of 'several Royal Academicians, disguised as artists'. The Austrian painter Josef Engelhart claimed that the first skirmish in the long campaign fought by the more advanced Vien-

The main entrance to the Paris Universal Exhibition of 1900 designed by René Binet. It was surmounted by *La Parisienne*, a sculpture of a contemporary woman in a Paquin robe by Moreau-Gauthier.

nese artists against the Künstlerhaus (the Austrian equivalent of the Royal Academy) took place in 1893, when the directors refused to exhibit his painting *The Cherry Picker* which showed a nude girl beneath some trees. The protests which the refusal provoked among the younger members of the Künstlerhaus led directly to the Vienna Secession.

An aspect of the official institutions of art in many European countries, which young artists and designers found particularly odious, was their unwillingness to accommodate exhibitions of the decorative (or applied) arts. All over Europe in the eighties and nineties artists formed societies in opposition to the ruling institutions. The new groups arranged exhibitions which not only featured modern painting and sculpture but also pottery, glass, furniture, metalwork and jewellery. In England, when the Royal Academy stubbornly refused to show works of decorative art, a rival body, the Art Workers' Guild, founded the Arts and Crafts Exhibition Society in 1888. In 1890 a group of French artists, including Rodin, disgruntled with the official Salon's conservative attitudes, founded the Société National des Beaux-Arts, whose annual exhibitions on the Champ de Mars in Paris included the decorative arts. The Secession groups, which broke away from the official artistic institutions in Berlin, Munich and Vienna, included architects and designers among their members. For instance, the painter and architect Peter Behrens was a co-founder of the Munich Secession which led to the formation in 1897 of the United Workshops for Art in Manufacture. The decorative arts were often displayed at the exhibitions organized by the Vienna Secession, and the Wiener Werkstätte (Vienna Workshops) were founded in 1903 by the architect Josef Hoffmann and the painter Kolo Moser, both members of the Secession.

GOTHIC AND ROCOCO INFLUENCES

In a review of the Universal Exhibition of 1889 in Paris, Louis de Fourcaud claimed that French taste had been 'finally emancipated from classical influences'. This was certainly an overstatement, but as the authority of the art establishment was undermined and full rein was given to the originality of artists and designers, the classical and Renaissance styles were overridden. 'The reign of the sacred Renaissance is over,' wrote the Belgian architect Paul Hankar in the magazine *L'Emulation*, reviewing an exhibition of paintings and decorative art from Glasgow which was held in Liège in 1895. 'It would be highly desirable,' he concluded, 'if this exhibition could be studied by all the directors of these drawing factories which we in Belgium call Academies of Fine Arts.' There was a degree of consensus among the artists who practised Art Nouveau that the Renaissance, and its revival of classicism, had nipped Gothic art in the bud, and that their task was to resuscitate the flower.

Sarah Bernhardt working on a self-portrait bust. The legendary actress was an accomplished amateur sculptress.

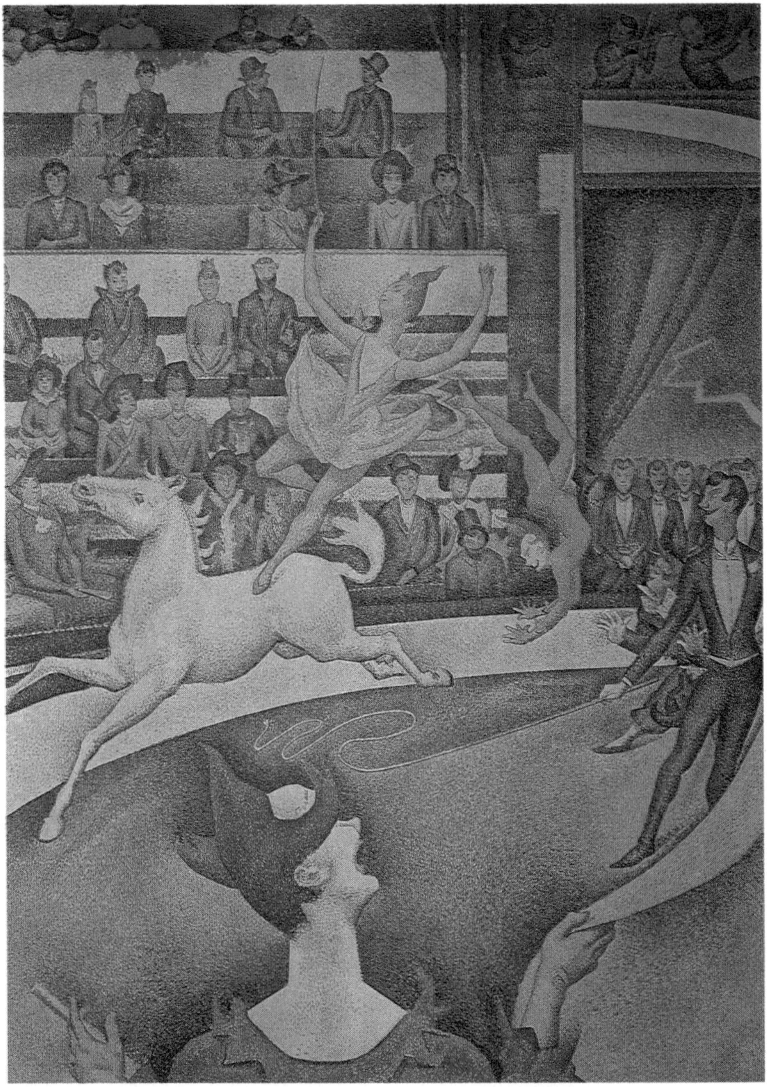

Georges Seurat: *The Circus*, 1891. This painting captures the gaiety and excitement of *la belle époque* and exploits the nervous energy of the whiplash line.

The French graphic artist Paul Berthon claimed that 'our new art is only.... the continuation and development of our *art de France* choked by the Renaissance. What we want is to create an original art.... following very closely the principles which made the medieval arts so thoroughly decorative.' The Catalan architect Antoni Gaudí (who designed the Sagrada Famiglia in Barcelona) lamented that the 'sublime' Gothic had been halted by the 'deplorable' Renaissance. He said: 'Today we must not imitate, or reproduce, but *continue* the Gothic....'

Many of the Art Nouveau artists spent the early years of their careers in neo-Gothic environments. Either, like William Morris and A.H. Mackmurdo, they worked in the offices of medievalist architects, or, like many of the Parisian designers, they frequented the night clubs of Montmartre. The writer and mystic Sâr

Cleo de Mérode, a celebrated Parisian courtesan, whose beauty inspired many artists.

Poster by Manuel Orazi advertising the gallery *La Maison Moderne* in Paris.

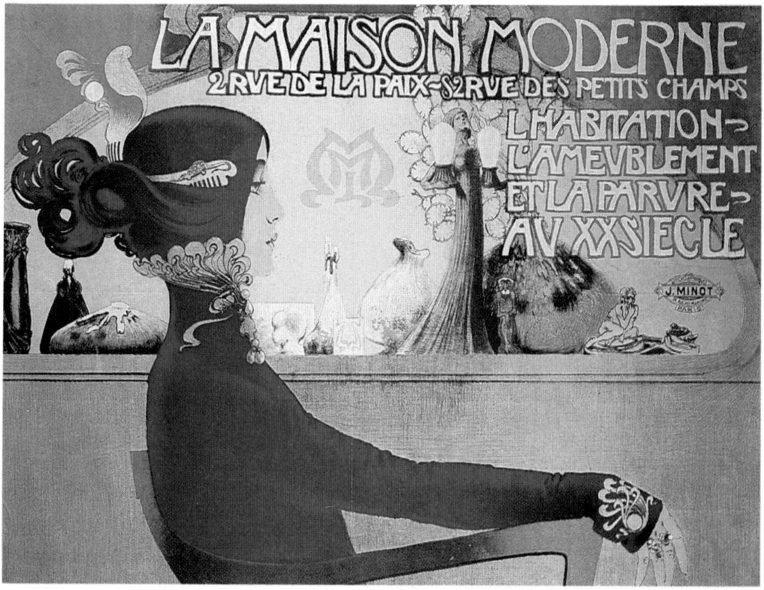

Péladan, describing the interior of Le Chat Noir, commented on 'two walls painted with frescoes', which showed 'some lively pseudo-medieval inventiveness', including a representation of Aristotle being burnt in effigy. The decoration of Le Chat Noir included drawings of cats by Théophile-Alexandre Steinlen, and the lantern which hung outside, adorned with snarling cats' heads, was designed by Eugène Grasset. The critic Gabriel Astruc, recalling another Montmartre night club, L'Abbaye de Thélème, wrote: 'Around 1885, decorators swore only by the ogive and the gargoyle.' Two aspects of Gothic art which are particularly noticeable in Art Nouveau are a predilection for vaulted construction (in architecture and furniture) and a fondness for the grotesque. Aubrey Beardsley's impish monsters and the repulsive masks created in stoneware pottery by Jean Carriès are direct descendants of the Gothic stonecarver's outlandish fantasy.

Rococo was another style with which several of the Art Nouveau designers had been familiar early in their careers, particularly those living in France where the Empress Eugénie had helped to revive eighteenth-century art and architecture. Emile Gallé, for example, began his career as a decorative artist designing neo-rococo ornament for china and glassware. Nancy, where Gallé worked, was rich in rococo masterpieces, and Art Nouveau designs which emanated from the city often displayed rococo elements, such as C- and S-scrolls and the consistent elimination of verticals and horizontals. Avoiding the right-angle became the preoccupation of several Art Nouveau designers. The Belgian architect Victor Horta designed some

The plaster sculpture of *La Parisienne* being lowered at the end of the 1900 Universal Exhibition in Paris.

of his buildings so that they appear not to have a single plumb vertical in their construction. Hector Guimard, the French architect who designed the entrances to the Paris Métro stations and who acknowledged Horta's influence, designed furniture which prompted the critic E. Moliner, writing in 1899, to compare him to the eighteenth-century *rocailleurs* (designers who worked in a fantastic style based on natural forms). Just as the original rococo had been a reaction against the bombastic classicism of the baroque, so Art Nouveau sought to break down the grandiose logic of the neo-classical and neo-Renaissance styles which prevailed during the second half of the nineteenth century.

ART NOUVEAU AND JAPAN

In 1874 J.K. Huysmans entitled one of his early prose poems *Rococo japonais*, thus neatly bracketing two significant influences on the Art Nouveau style. The painter James McNeill Whistler concluded his 'Ten o'clock' lecture, delivered in 1885, with these words: '....the story of the beautiful is already complete – hewn in the marbles of the Parthenon – and broidered, with the birds, upon the fan of Hokusai – at the foot of Fusiyama.' To suggest a parity between the sculptors of ancient Greece and the decorative arts of nineteenth-century Japan was, as Whistler well knew, mischievously provocative, but it was certainly accurate in terms of the influence the two styles were to have on Western art over the next twenty years. It was further suggested that Japanese art would help undo the damage inflicted by the Renaissance on European art. In an article which appeared in the last issue of the Boston periodical *The Knight Errant*, published in 1893, the American painter Arthur W. Dow asserted: 'All Japanese artists were designers; the same was true of European artists until the Renaissance.'

Portrait of Edmond de Goncourt by Félix Bracquemond. The celebrated novelist and critic was an informed collector of Japanese art.

In 1854 Commodore Matthew Perry opened up Japan to trade with the West, and soon objects of Japanese art were reaching the ports of Europe and the USA. The French artist Félix Bracquemond discovered some leaves of Hokusai's *Manga* being used as wrapping paper in 1856, and in 1858 textiles decorated with designs based on Japanese prints were being mass produced in Manchester, England. Examples of the decorative arts of Japan were shown at international exhibitions in London (1862), Paris (1867 and 1878) and Philadelphia (1876). Western collectors accumulated detailed historical and technical information about Japanese art, and well-illustrated monographs were published. In 1875 *Keramik Art of Japan* by George Ashdown Audsley and James Lord Bowes appeared; Ernest Chesnau published *Le Japon à Paris* in 1878, and he gave lectures on Japanese art at the Union des Arts Décoratifs (the forerunner of the Musée des Arts Décoratifs) in Paris. The English designer Dr Christopher

The Casa Mila, a block of apartments in Barcelona designed by the Catalan architect Antoni Gaudí.

Dresser contributed *Japan, its Architecture, Art and Art Manufactures* in 1882, a book based on the author's visit to the country five years earlier. In 1883 Louis Gonse, editor of the *Gazette des Beaux-Arts*, published his two-volume *L'Art japonais*, and the same year a massive exhibition of Japanese art from public and private collections was held at the Union Centrale. In 1886 the American archaeologist and zoologist Edward S. Morse published at Boston *Japanese Homes and their Surroundings*, an illustrated book which profoundly affected American architecture and interior decoration.

The chapter on ceramics in Gonse's book had been contributed by Siegfried Bing, an important collector of, and dealer in, Japanese *objets d'art*. From 1888 to 1891 Bing published the periodical *Le Japon Artistique* which also appeared in an English language version called *Artistic Japan*. During the 1880s and 1890s copies of the Japanese illustrated art magazine *Koku-Kwa* were circulated in Europe.

In the first issue of *Le Japon Artistique*, Siegfried Bing described Japanese art as an '*art nouveau*' which would have a deep and lasting effect on Western design. The use of Japanese motifs as decorative designs on all sorts of objects from textiles to ceramics during the 1860s and 1870s, was followed in the 1880s by a more thorough assimilation of the principles on which Japanese art was based. Rookwood and Copenhagen ceramics, Gallé glass and Tiffany metalwork were all decorated according to these principles. The most significant lesson learnt from Japanese art by Western designers was a refined asymmetry in the arrangement of quite different elements on a two-dimensional surface, which superseded the symmetrical and perspectival compositions in an illusory three-dimensional space, normal in European decorative art ever since the Renaissance.

Another aspect of Japanese art which was readily taken on board by many Western artists was the way in which nature was treated. Ruskin had urged artists to study nature minutely and to copy her exactly. But many artists had considered it desirable to paraphrase nature in the interests of design. In his 'Ten o'clock' lecture, Whistler said:

'Nature is very rarely right, to such an extent even, that it might almost be said that Nature is usually wrong: that is to say, the condition of things that shall bring about the perfection of harmony worth a picture is rare, and not common at all.' In 1899 Berthon expressed similar ideas and started by indicating his inspiration: 'The Japanese artists nowadays treat the plants, the landscapes, the animals, everything even the clouds, in a decorative manner. I myself only try to copy nature in its very essence. If I want to use a plant as decoration I am not going to reproduce all the nerves of its leaves or the exact tint of its flowers.'

James McNeill Whistler: *Nocturne in Blue and Gold, Old Battersea Bridge*. This painting shows the influence of Japanese woodblock prints on Whistler.

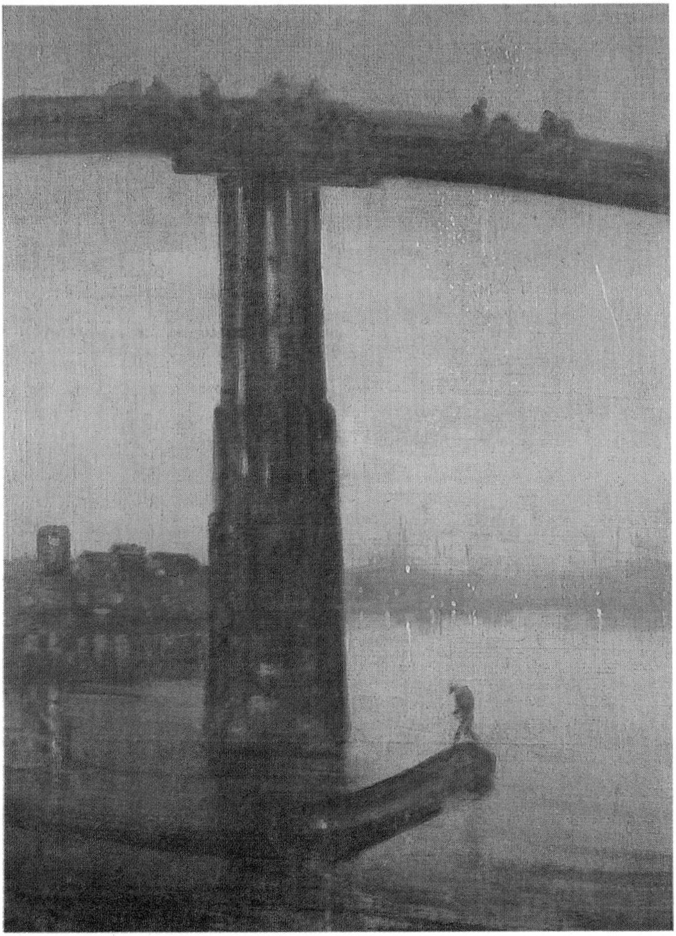

NATURE AS SYMBOL

Art Nouveau artists used nature to symbolize a state of mind or an intellectual concept. For example, some designers used motifs from marine biology to express the Darwinian theory of evolution. The English architect C.F.A. Voysey created a wallpaper showing a water-snake swimming through reeds. He gave the snake wing-like fins, and the image relates to the research of the biologist Thomas Huxley who had tried to demonstrate the evolution of some reptiles into birds. In Munich, August Endell designed the Elvira studio in 1897, which he adorned inside and out with motifs taken from marine biology. Two years later the biologist Ernst Haeckel published his *Kunstformen der Natur* (Art forms in nature); the illustrations are drawings of the lower forms of life that were particularly the subject of biologists' scrutiny at that time. René Binet, architect of the principal gateway to the 1900 Universal Exhibition in Paris, confessed to studying the plates in Haeckel's volume.

Alternatively, artists working in the Art Nouveau style used nature to provide symbols which evoked a psychological mood. There were close links between Art Nouveau and the Symbolist movement in literature and drama. The actress Sarah Bernhardt, herself a sculptress, ordered jewellery from Lalique; posters advertising her performances were designed by Alphonse Mucha. The glass artist Emile Gallé inscribed lines from Symbolist poetry on some of his pieces. The Scottish architect Charles Rennie Mackintosh designed a music-room for Fritz Wärndorfer in Vienna which was decorated with motifs drawn from Maurice Maeterlinck's *Seven Princesses*. Sometimes the current flowed the other way. The Symbolist poet Léon Bloy wrote a set of twelve verses as a commentary on Eugène Grasset's designs for a calendar, and a ring by René Lalique plays a significant role in Jean Lorrain's novel *L'Aryenne*.

THE SPIRIT OF REVOLT

Writers and artists were perplexed during the second half of the nineteenth century by the emerging female psyche. Greater comprehension of female sexuality was blurred by a growing anxiety about women's campaign for equality. In H.G. Wells's novel *Ann Veronica*, one of the male characters asserts: 'Since the girls of the eighties broke bounds and sailed away on bicycles.... it's been one triumphant relaxation.' Bicycle posters of *la belle époque* reveal as much about the emancipation of women as any feminist tract. Most of them show carefree girls whose new-found mobility has induced in them a happy, even ecstatic, abandon. Makes of bicycles were given names like 'Papillon' (Butterfly), 'Déesse' (Goddess) and 'Liberator'. At the Paris Universal Exhibition of 1900 there was a Palais de la Femme which was supposed to demonstrate through effigies of famous women from the Empress Theodora to Harriet Beecher Stowe that, as the official catalogue claimed, 'woman can raise herself to the level of man and emulate him in his achievements'.

A couple dancing the tango. The craze for the Argentinian dance was discouraged by most of the European potentates before the First World War.

Jean Béraud: *The Chalet du Cycle in the Bois de Boulogne.* The bicycle proved very popular during the 1890s, particularly among the more emancipated women in France and Britain.

Another male gesture of conciliation offered at the Exhibition of 1900 was to place on top of Binet's gateway *La Parisienne,* a plaster statue by Moreau-Gauthier of a self-assured, contemporary woman in a robe created by Paquin. It was regarded by the man (if not the woman) in the street as symbolizing the triumph of prostitution; besides, after the exhibition it was dismantled.

The female demanding equal rights was often regarded by the increasingly insecure male as a virago. In 1868 the Goncourt brothers noted in their journal that the Belgian painter Félicien Rops was 'truly eloquent in depicting the cruel aspect of contemporary woman, her steely glance, and her malevolence towards man, not hidden, not disguised, but evident in the whole of her person'. An alternative to such a bristlingly defensive attitude was the patronizing sympathy offered by the Austrian writer Peter Altenberg in 1902: commenting in *Ver Sacrum,* the periodical of the Vienna Secession, on *Mother and Child,* a painting by the Dutch artist Jan Toorop, he observed: 'What a terrible tragedy for a noble organism, to have to give forth its best powers for procreation and childbirth.'

Walter Crane's *Flora's Feast,* a book of coloured woodcuts depicting flowers as women, was a naively conceived catalogue of symbolic representations which inspired Art Nouveau artists in Europe and

America. Crane's botanical beauties echoed Richard Wagner's flower-maidens in his *Parsifal* of 1882, whose ensnaring lust the hero victoriously resists. Wagner's music-dramas became a cult among the intelligentsia, and Bayreuth a place of pilgrimage. Wagner societies were founded in most European capitals, and in Paris *La Revue wagnérienne* was one of the principal organs of Symbolism during the 1880s. What was attractive about Wagner's music was the way in which it contained the chaotic forces of emotion and desire within an orderly, more cerebral structure. At a less exalted level, Art Nouveau designers were often striving after the same effect. William Morris stated that the aim of textile design was 'to combine clearness of form and firmness of structure with the mystery that comes of abundance and richness of detail.'

Henry van de Velde described nature as 'disorderly and chaotic', and he developed an abstract style based on what he called the 'dynamographic' line. In 1900 he settled in Berlin, and his theories on the decorative arts were influential throughout Germany. In Austria the designers of the Wiener Werkstätte worked in their own abstract style which was predominantly geometrical. Form and pattern were composed of squares, circles and triangles. It was a style remarkably different from the flowers and tendrils that covered so much Art Nouveau of the 1880s and 1890s and was a far cry from the sensual ladies drawn by Walter Crane, Eugène Grasset and Alphonse Mucha. It cannot be confused or compared with the springing curves and vaulted structures of Victor Horta's buildings or Henry van de Velde's furniture. But it has in common with all Art Nouveau the element of revolt. It was brazenly unconventional, an affront to public taste if not a danger to public morals. For the new century was no less prudish than the old; propriety still had its day. Whereas in 1882 a commentator writing in *Le Figaro* had attributed the 'loosening of morals in France and the decay of the family' to the effects of the 'dissolute quadrille', thirty years later it was the tango which raised the ire of the Kaiser, the Tsar and the Pope.

In 1914 Europe plunged itself into the blood-bath of the First World War, perhaps more in the hope of resolving moral dilemmas than to settle the scores of *realpolitik*. 'So crumble away society!' Des Essientes had cried, and he had continued: 'Perish old world!'

Illustration by Walter Crane to his book *Flora's Feast*. The identification of women with flowers was characteristic of the Art Nouveau style.

CHAPTER ONE

GLASS

Gallé etched and enamelled bowl.
Sold: Bonham's, London, 27/6/86.
Price: £880.

Gallé cameo vase
Height: 15.6cm
Ursula, P16 Antiquarius, London
Price: £650

Art Nouveau glass falls into two principal categories: cameo and iridescent. Though quite different in technique and appearance, the two types shared a restrained quality, which was much favoured by *fin de siècle* connoisseurs; the beauty of both is less obvious than the sparkle of the cut crystal produced at that time, and their colours are softer than the ruby, yellow or blue flashed glass that was so popular towards the end of the nineteenth century.

Another factor that cameo and iridescent glass had in common was the sophistication of the techniques employed in their manufacture. Late nineteenth-century artists were very arrogant. They liked to think they could achieve anything that their forebears had centuries before, and a lot of time was spent rediscovering the so-called 'secrets' of earlier craftsmen. The polychrome glazing of the French Renaissance potter Palissy and medieval enamelling were two of the many processes revived by nineteenth-century artisans. Emulating ancient techniques was often the motive behind historicism in the arts, as much as any philosophical, political or religious nostalgia for times gone by. Ancient Roman cameo-cut glass was imitated because it was a technological challenge rather than in memory of a golden age. Similarly, the iridescence on glass dug up by archaeologists aroused the scientific curiosity of many nineteenth-century glassmakers, who reproduced the effect in their workshops. They wanted to show that in addition to anything their ancestors had achieved they could also do what previously only Nature had been able to do.

CAMEO GLASS IN ENGLAND

The technique of producing cameo glass consists of making a vessel in two or more layers of differently coloured glass. The outer layers are carved in relief, and the ornamental design then stands out in the colour of its layer against the colour of the inner layer. Cameo glass was made in the first centuries BC and AD. One of the finest examples of Roman cameo glass, the Portland Vase, was reproduced in pottery by Josiah Wedgwood during the 1780s; forty-five copies were made. Some seventy years later the Staffordshire glassmaker Benjamin Richardson showed his decorating staff one of these Wedgwood vases, and offered £1,000 to the first man who could make a copy in glass.

A craftsman called John Northwood took up the challenge and after years of painstaking experiments and heart-breaking failures, he finally succeeded in 1877. Northwood was immediately commissioned to execute other cameo glass vases, including one for Thomas Webb & Sons, a firm of Staffordshire glassmakers. In 1882 Northwood became art director of Stevens & Williams, another Staffordshire firm, and these two factories supplied a growing demand for cameo glass over the next twenty years. However, the designs on the cameo glass produced by Thomas Webb and Steven & Williams were usually mythological or floral and only occasionally related to Art Nouveau. To increase production, both firms used hydrofluoric acid to etch the decoration roughly which was then finished with the engraving wheel; the backgrounds were polished on high-speed lathes.

Richard cameo vase
Height: 25.1cm
Ursula, P16 Antiquarius, London
Price: £550

FRENCH STYLES

The significance of English cameo glass lay in the influence it exerted on Emile Gallé, when he saw it exhibited at the Paris Universal Exhibition of 1878. In that year Gallé was thirty-two, and he was running his father's glassworks in Nancy. Before that he had spent two years at Weimar University where he had studied mineralogy, art history and botany. From 1864 to 1868 he had worked at the glassworks of Burgun, Schverer & Co. in Meisenthal, near Nancy, a firm which decorated some of the glass made at the Gallé factory. The defeat of France in the Franco-Prussian War (in which Gallé fought) left Meisenthal in the hands of the Germans.

Gallé had returned to Nancy in 1873, when he established a small glass workshop. The glass that he manufactured during the 1870s had been transparent – either colourless or softly tinted – and was known as *clair de lune*. Shapes had been classical or traditional, and the enamel decoration inspired by the French rococo style made popular during the 1860s by the Empress Eugénie. At the Paris Universal Exhibition of 1878 Gallé was awarded a gold medal for his *clair de lune* glass, but his pride in this achievement was overwhelmed by his admiration for the work of some of his contemporaries, particularly the carved cameo glass made by John Northwood in England.

During the 1880s Gallé experimented with a wide range of decorative techniques. Impressed also by the glass that François Eugène Rousseau had exhibited in 1878, Gallé began to make layered glass with coloured crystals and pieces of gold, platinum or silver leaf trapped between the layers, a technique called 'intercalary' decoration. On Gallé's glass the outer layer was often cameo-carved, and sometimes the inner layer was made of opaque glass in imitation of hardstones. Many pieces were made of more than two layers, the carving varying in depth to form subtle, multicoloured decorative designs. A variety of means were employed to effect the relief patterns – hydrofluoric acid, wheel-carving and small chisels.

As well as his technique, Gallé's style also underwent a transformation. Always a keen amateur botanist, he began to use plant motifs more and more in the decoration of his glass in the 1880s. The particular treatment that he gave to plant forms was considerably influenced by Japanese art. Gallé must have been aware of the decorative arts of Japan for many years before, but at this time he had a close friendship with Tokuoso Takashima, a Japanese botanical artist who from 1885 to 1888 was a student at the School of Forestry in Nancy. Takashima taught Gallé the Oriental way of holding a paintbrush; when Henri Frantz, writing in *The Magazine of Art* in 1897, tried to belittle Gallé's debt to Japanese art he unwittingly indicated its full extent: 'He seems to condense the whole motive of a plant, to give it an attitude.... to draw out its individuality in a very living way....' Frantz expresses here what is virtually the aesthetic of Zen Buddhism.

Another influence on the style of Gallé's glass was Symbolism. 'Consciously or unconsciously,' he said, 'the symbol qualifies the work of art and makes it live; it is its soul.' He regarded Nature as a thesaurus of symbols. According to Symbolist theory, flowers, insects or animals do not necessarily represent something else, but they should always contribute to the evocation of a mood or a thought in the spectator's mind. To amplify such an evocation, Gallé sometimes incorporated lines of poetry in the decoration of his glass; he often quoted Hugo, Baudelaire or Maeterlinck. Towards the end of the 1880s Gallé met the poet Robert de Montesquiou who not only encouraged the artist's appreciation of Symbolism but also introduced his glass to Parisian high society. With such wealthy patronage, it was feasible to

Daum cameo vase
Height: 11.5cm
Sold: Sotheby's, London, 16/5/86
Price: £550

lavish almost unlimited artistic talent and technical skill on each piece of glass. Auguste Legras, a leading contemporary glass manufacturer, was prompted to comment: 'Gallé's product.... is true art glass, dream glass, poetic glass, whatever you like to call it except commercial glass.'

Gallé reacted to such criticism and began to manufacture much cheaper cameo glass. Using two-layered vessels, the decoration was cut out entirely with hydrofluoric acid, using templates so that the pattern could be repeated many times. The ratio of retail prices for handmade examples of Gallé glass to those for industrial pieces has been reckoned to have been at least sixty to one. Nowadays, the difference is generally much less, although handmade Gallé glass has become prohibitively expensive over the last few years and only industrial examples are reasonably affordable. But many of the smaller, cheaper pieces, decorated with acid-cut designs of plants or landscape in two-layered opaque, coloured glass, are most attractive. Industrial Gallé glass, although lacking the artistic merit, technical élan and Symbolist overtones of the best handmade examples, are nevertheless charming mementoes of the *fin de siècle*, and are quintessentially Art Nouveau.

Between 1890 and 1910 Gallé's cameo-carved glass was imitated far and wide. Burgun, Schverer & Co. was one of the earliest firms to copy the new ware. A technical variation developed by this factory was to paint the decorative design on the inner layer and then cover this with an outer layer of transparent glass; when this was carved, it produced the illusion of more layers of glass than had actually been used. The chief designer from 1885 was Désiré Christian who left in 1896 to set up his own workshop.

In the mid-1890s the Muller brothers established a glass decorating workshop in Lunéville (five of the nine brothers had worked for Gallé). There they developed a technique called 'fluorgravure'; as well as cameo-carving decorative designs in multi-layered vases, some areas of the glass were covered with enamels which were vitrified and then etched with hydrofluoric acid. During 1906 and 1907 two of the Muller brothers,

Daum cameo vase
Height: 28.5cm
Sold: Bonham's, London, 5/12/86
Price: £748

02-1105

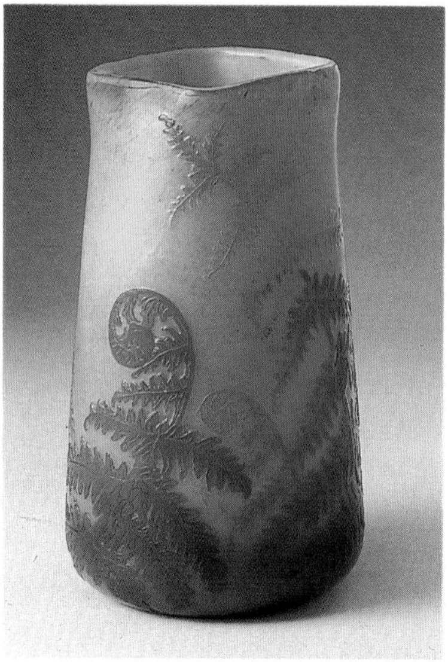

Legras cameo vase
Height: 17.4cm
Ursula, P16 Antiquarius, London
Price: £395

Désiré and Henri, were employed by the Val St Lambert glassworks in Belgium, where they produced a series of vases in the 'fluorgravure' technique.

Paul Nicolas worked at Gallé's factory from 1893 to 1918 and at the same time made cameo-carved glass in his own workshop. Charles Vessière was another independent glass artist who worked in the Nancy area making cameo-carved vases.

In 1878 Jean Daum bought a glassworks in Nancy from a partnership unable to repay money that it had borrowed from him – he knew nothing about either the manufacture or distribution of glassware. After a year he was joined by his son Auguste who contrived to put the enterprise on a sound financial footing. His second son Antonin started working for the firm in 1887, and during a period of convalescence in 1890 he sketched some vases with floral decoration which were successfully executed in the factory. The following year decorating studios were opened and the firm began to produce large quantities of cameo glass.

The decorative designs carved on Daum's glass are generally close to Gallé's in that plants, insects and landscapes prevail, but it is perhaps true to say that Daum's floral designs lack the Oriental vitality that characterize Gallé's draughtsmanship. The Daum factory developed two processes for giving the inner, background layer of glass an interesting surface texture. With the decoration masked, some vases were submerged in hydrofluoric acid which gave the backgrounds a frosted appearance. Alternatively, the inner layer was wheel-cut with small, circular facets which made the background look as if it had been hammered, much like beaten copper.

Another process developed by Daum was called 'vitrification'. The vessel, still hot, was rolled in ground glass of a different colour. When it was reheated the ground glass vitrified into a thin outer layer, and the decoration was then hand-carved or acid-cut. Greater depth, and further colour, might then be added by applying a pastille of glass over a coloured insert; this was then carved to form, for instance, the body of an insect or the corolla of a flower.

Other glassworks in Alsace-Lorraine making cameo glass were Vallérystal, Saint Louis and Baccarat. Saint Louis cameo glass was acid-cut with hardly ever any carving, and it is marked 'St Louis-Munzthal', 'D'Argental' (the French name for Munzthal) or 'Arsall'. Cameo-glass vases made by Vallérystal are generally blue-grey, overlaid with dark red; the designers who worked for the firm included Otto Krüger and Bruno Paul, both founder members of the Vereinigte Werkstätten (United Workshops) in Munich.

Some factories in the Paris region also produced cameo glass. Camille Tutré de Varreux made vases for the Pantin glassworks which are signed 'De Vez'. The firm of Legras used the frosting and vitrification techniques developed by Daum, and also manufactured multi-layered glass which was cameo-cut and enamelled to give the appearance of carved cornelian. Cameo glass was made in Paris at the workshops of Ernest-Baptiste Léveillé, and the painter Henri Laurent-Desrousseaux designed vases and bowls, cameo-carved with floral decoration, for Jules Mabut's Verrerie de la Paix. Louis Damon, who had a shop on the boulevard Malesherbes, bought cased glass blanks manufacutured by Daum to his own design which were then cameo- and intaglio-carved in his own workshops.

OTHER CAMEO-GLASS MANUFACTURERS

In Germany, Ferdinand von Poschinger's glassworks at Buchenau, Bavaria, and the china and glassware manufacturers Villeroy & Boch, produced cameo glass in imitation of Gallé's work although never attaining the quality of anything more exalted than his industrial glass.

Several of the Bohemian glassworks made cameo glass, including

Bohemian enamelled vase
Height: 22.8cm
Ursula, P16 Antiquarius, London
Price: £280

Harrach, Goldberg, Wilhelm Kralik Sohn, Reich & Co. of Krasna, Moser of Karlsbad, Heckert of Petersdorf and Loetz of Klöstermühle.

In Sweden, the Kosta and Reijmyre factories produced cameo glass. Alf Wallander designed for both and Gunnar Wennerberg for Kosta. Some of the Reijmyre cameo vases, decorated with designs of flowers, dragonflies or submarine life, and incorporating coloured streaks, air bubbles and spirals, are of estimable quality. When the Orrefors glassworks started making art glass in 1913, cameo glass manufactured in the style of Gallé was among its earliest products.

The Imperial Russian Glassworks

in St Petersburg manufactured cameo glass decorated with designs influenced by the work of the Reijmyre and Kosta artists.

In America the Steuben factory at Corning, New York, incorporated in 1903, made what was called 'acid cut-back' glass, using the technique employed on industrial Gallé glass. Cameo glass was also made at the Honesdale Decorating Company in Pennsylvania.

IRIDESCENT GLASS AND ITS ORIGINS

Nineteenth-century glassworkers were fascinated by the iridescence on ancient glass which was dug up by archaeologists. The effect is due to carbonic acid in the soil which, over the centuries, breaks up the surface of the glass which becomes layered; light rays falling on it are split creating a prismatic appearance. Large amounts of such glass were being excavated in the Near East in the 1870s, particularly as the Turkish empire became more accessible to archaeologists. The Congress of Berlin gave Cyprus to Britain in 1878; Tiffany named a type of his iridescent glass 'Cypriote' and Fritz Heckert's glassworks in Bohemia manufactured iridescent glass called 'Cyperngläser'. Similarly, the Loetz firm made 'Kreta' iridescent glass, and the Steuben Glass Works in America produced 'Tyrian'.

Gallé cameo vase
Height: 20.25cm
Sold: Sotheby's, London, 16/5/86
Price: £880

The iridescent glass manufactured during the last quarter of the nineteenth century was produced by coating coloured glass with metallic oxides. The Austrian firm of Lobmeyr exhibited examples at the Vienna Exhibition of 1873. The development of the technique might have remained a scientific curiosity had it not been for the great and widespread publicity given to the discoveries of the archaeologist Heinrich Schliemann. His book *Troy and its remains*, published in 1875, tells the story of his excavation of the sites mentioned in Homer's *Iliad*. The following year, Schliemann made his sensational discoveries at Mycenae. Partly as the result of the current popularity of archaeology, the Paris Exhibition of 1878 featured modern iridescent glass manufactured by Lobmeyr, Thomas Webb & Son and the Pantin glassworks. The style of these wares was not Art Nouveau, nor did any of these firms persist to any great extent in the production of iridescent glass, but their displays inspired other glassworkers. In the

Muller Frères cut and enamelled vase
Height: 40.5cm
Sold: Sotheby's Arcade, New York, 19/6/86
Price: $1045

early 1880s Louis Comfort Tiffany, whose glass factory was making coloured glass for windows and lampshades, began experimenting with iridescence, and during the same decade the Austrian firm of Bakalowits started production.

AUSTRIAN DESIGNS

In 1890 the Loetz glassworks of Klöstermühle in South Bohemia, whose principal retailer in Vienna was Bakalowits, introduced its own iridescent glass. The firm's managing director Max von Spaun concentrated research on the technique, and patents were taken out. In 1898, Loetz held an exhibition in Vienna showing examples of iridescent glass designed by von Spaun.

Loetz manufactured numerous different sorts of iridescent glass, but the two principal types were 'Papillon' and 'Phenomenon'. On Papillon glass, iridescent spots cover the vessel; Phenomenon is iridescent glass decorated with glass threads

De Vez cameo vase
Height: 31cm
Sold: Sotheby's Arcade, New York, 19/6/86
Price: $990

Bronze lamp with leaded glass shade
Height: 57cm
Sold: Christie's South Kensington, London, 19/9/86
Price: £770

pulled into wavy lines. Some of the shapes are quite conventional, but others are dramatically waisted or pinched. Handles have sometimes been applied. Maria Kirschner and Adolf Beckert were the two main designers for Loetz, but there were several outside artists who also supplied designs, including many of the Wiener Werkstätte designers, particularly Kolo Moser.

Not all Loetz glass is marked. When it is, it tends to be expensive. Unmarked Loetz is not always easy to differentiate from the work of numerous imitators. Experience alone can provide confident attribution. However, most of the European manufacturers who tried to imitate Loetz's iridescent glass did not achieve anything like the richness or variety of colours of the original. Bakalowits followed the example of Loetz and commissioned designs for iridescent glass from avant-garde Viennese designers including Kolo Moser and one of his pupils, Jutta Sika.

As soon as iridescent glass became wildly popular, most of the leading Bohemian glassworks climbed on the bandwagon. Harrach, Goldberg, Kralik, Heckert and Pallme König all manufactured the ware, and the products of the different firms are extremely difficult to identify. In Germany, von Poschinger made iridescent glass, as did Josef Emil Schneckendorf, a sculptor in Munich who, in about 1898, started experimenting with glass. He established his own workshop where he produced iridescent glass, sometimes in floral shapes. From 1907 to 1911 he was director of the Grand-Ducal Glassworks at Darmstadt where he continued to design iridescent wares.

IRIDESCENT GLASS IN AMERICA

Louis Comfort Tiffany's entry into the field of iridescent glass seems to have been quite independent of developments at the Loetz factory. He had experimented with iridescence during the 1880s and when he opened a new glassworks at Corona, Long Island, in 1893, production of iridescent glass was soon under way. Tiffany's iridescent glass was probably the finest made in the Art Nouveau style. It was expensive to produce; a small proportion of Loetz's output, for instance gooseneck flasks, was imitation-Tiffany which sold at a much lower price than the real thing. Some of Tiffany's decorative *tours de force* were the techniques of pulling iridescent glass threads into feather formations and shaping blobs of iridescent glass into the form of, for example, a lily-pad or a poppy. 'Cypriote' glass was given a pitted surface and decorated with iridescent flowers or leaves. 'Lava' glass was cratered and decorated with trails of gold iridescent glass. Examples of these special decorative effects are very expensive today. The plainer gold or blue iridescent glass, particularly tableware, is generally cheaper and sets of wine or liqueur glasses, in good Art Nouveau shapes, are often sold at quite moderate prices. Lamps with Tiffany iridescent glass shades are not as expensive as those with the leaded glass shades, but are nevertheless beyond the reach of the average collector.

From 1901, the Quezal Art Glass and Decorating Company of Brooklyn, New York, produced a precise imitation of Tiffany's iridescent glass. Quezal was run by Martin Bach who

Iridescent vase
Height: 8.9cm
Ursula, P16 Antiquarius, London
Price: £45

Loetz iridescent vase (unsigned)
Height: 15.9cm
Sold: Christie's South Kensington, London, 25/7/86
Price: £420

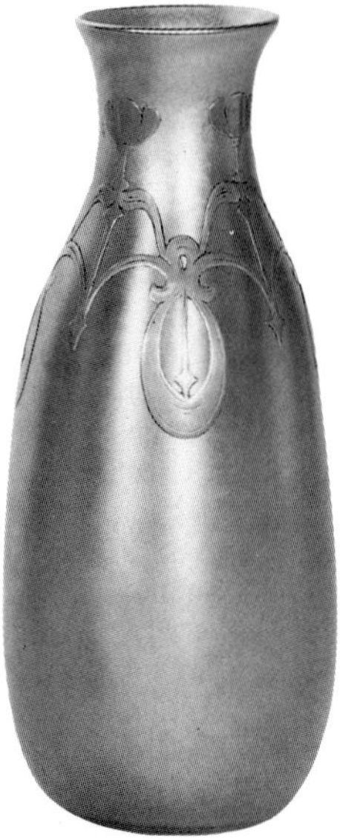

Quezal iridescent vase
Height: 22.8cm
Sold: Christie's South Kensington, London, 25/7/86
Price: £400

had worked at the Corona factory, and he hired other technicians who had been employed by Tiffany. Neither Quezal-produced glass nor 'Kew-Blas', a similar line of iridescent glass manufactured by the Union Glass Co. of Somerville, Massachusetts, has the subtlety or refinement of Tiffany's ware, but examples of both are sometimes very beautiful and comparatively inexpensive. Other notable companies were the Steuben Glass Works, which made iridescent glass called 'Aurene', the Fenton Art Glass Co. of Martin's Ferry, Ohio, and the Fostoria glassworks of Fostoria, also in Ohio, which both produced poor imitations of Tiffany's iridescent glass.

Some of the drinking glasses produced by Tiffany were in the shape of flowers, a particularly Art Nouveau concept. Josef Schneckendorf in Munich also made iridescent glasses in the form of flowers, inspired by the designs of Karl Koepping. Koepping worked in Berlin with Friedrich Zitzmann, a glass-blower who had gained experience at a Murano glassworks; from 1896 Koepping made drinking glasses with cups in the form of flower heads on long, thin stems which had glass leaves and even tendrils apparently growing out of them. They were quite unfunctional and very fragile; few have survived.

The London firm of James Powell & Sons made drinking glasses in the shape of flowers, most of them in clear glass with streaks of opalescent yellow.

GLASS TABLEWARE

Many of the leading Art Nouveau designers worked for glass manufacturers, supplying designs for tableware. The Dutch architect H.P. Berlage was commissioned by both the Pantin and Baccarat glassworks in France to design shapes for drinking glasses, decanters and jugs, and Ferdinand von Poschinger manufactured table glass at Buchenau to designs by the Munich artists Adalbert Niemeyer and Richard Riemerschmid. The Rheinische Glashütten at Cologne-Ehrenfeld produced tableware from designs by Kolo Moser, the architect Peter Behrens, Gisela Falke von Lilienstein (one of Josef Hoffmann's

Tiffany iridescent vase *left*
Height: 22.7cm
Sold: Sotheby's Arcade, New York, 19/6/86
Price: $1100

Quezal iridescent vase *centre*
Height: 14.5cm
Sold: Sotheby's Arcade, New York, 19/6/86
Price: $880

Tiffany iridescent vase (unsigned) *right*
Height: 28cm
Sold: Sotheby's Arcade, New York, 19/6/86
Price: $715

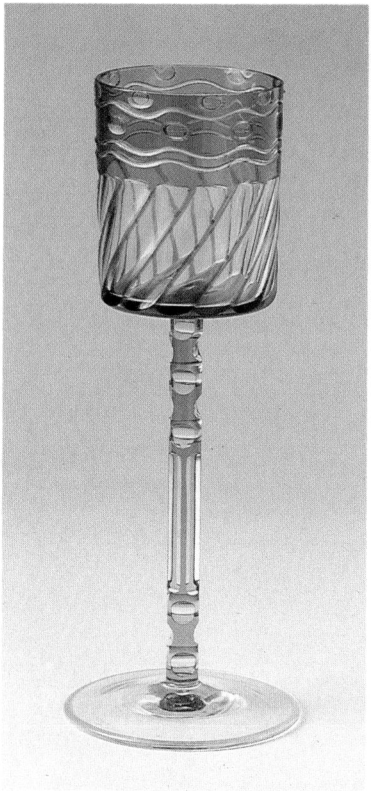

Goblet designed by Otto Prutscher
Height: 22.5cm
Andrew Lineham Antiques,
T5/6 Antiquarius, London
Price: £1000

Pallme König iridescent vase
Height: 44.8cm
Andrew Lineham Antiques,
T5/6 Antiquarius, London
Price: £950

pupils) and others. The artist Hans Christiansen designed tableware for the Theresientaler Krystallglasfabrik.

In Austria the firm of Lobmeyr commissioned designs for shapes and decoration from several members of the Wiener Werkstätte including, most notably, Otto Prutscher and Josef Hoffmann. The latter also supplied Lobmeyr's with repeating patterns which were painted in black or dark grey on clear glass vessels. This was called 'bronzite' decoration; Ludwig Heinrich Jungnickel produced designs of stylized animals and birds for application by the same technique. Bakalowits manufactured tableware designed by Kolo Moser and the Austrian architect Joseph Maria Olbrich.

In France, an American artist, Edward Colonna, designed glasses and decanters for Siegfried Bing's gallery La Maison de l'Art Nouveau in Paris. Another designer who worked extensively for Bing was Georges de Feure who designed shapes for two glass vases and a glass pitcher, which were produced in large quantities, although they were not, apparently, sold at Bing's shop.

The English designer Dr Christopher Dresser worked for the Glasgow firm of James Couper & Sons, but his designs were for art glass rather than tableware. 'Clutha', as this glass was called, was free-blown in shapes derived from classical and primitive art. It was decorated internally with wisps of white or coloured glass, inclusions of silver foil, air bubbles, and sometimes patches of aventurine. Clutha glass which bears Dresser's mark is more expensive than unsigned pieces. Some Clutha glass was designed by the Scottish architect George Walton; his shapes are more restrained and more

elegant, and the decoration is usually limited to opaque white streaks and air bubbles in clear, green glass. Pieces designed by Walton were not marked and tend to be quite inexpensive. Some Liberty's Tudric pewter is lined with Clutha glass, and a Clutha rosebowl was designed for a Tudric mount. Thomas Webb & Sons made glass called 'Old Roman' which was sufficiently close to Clutha for Couper's to complain of plagiarism.

PÂTE DE VERRE

No survey of Art Nouveau glass would be complete without mention of *pâte de verre*, a cross between glass and pottery. It was made from powdered glass mixed with metal oxides to give colour, and a liquid binding agent; it was then fired like pottery. The material was developed by the French artist Henri Cros, and others who used it were Albert Dammouse, François Décorchemont, Almaric Walter (who ran a studio at the Daum factory making *pâte de verre*) and the Belgian Georges Despret. Today, only Despret's work is affordable; pieces by the other artists tend to be savagely fought over in the saleroom.

Tiffany iridescent vase
Height: 21.75cm
Sold: Phillips, London, 13/3/86
Price: £462

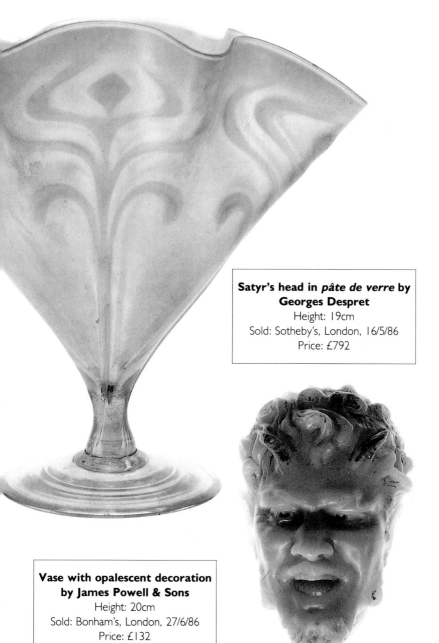

Satyr's head in *pâte de verre* by Georges Despret
Height: 19cm
Sold: Sotheby's, London, 16/5/86
Price: £792

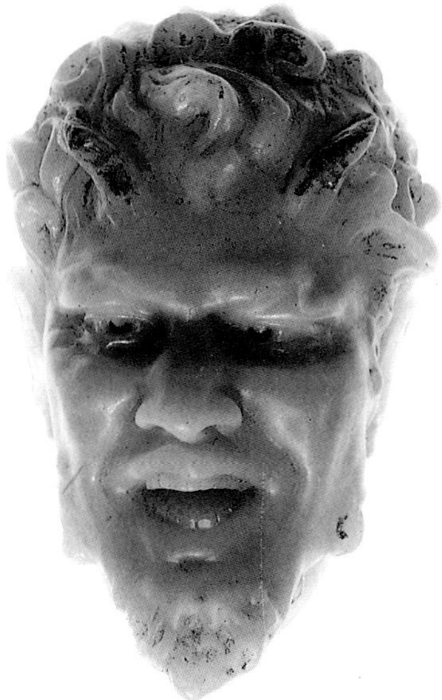

Vase with opalescent decoration by James Powell & Sons
Height: 20cm
Sold: Bonham's, London, 27/6/86
Price: £132

Object	Quality of manufacture	Quality of design and/or decoration	Rarity	Price (£)	Price ($)
Anon.					
iridescent vase	6	7	■	40–250	60–400
leaded glass lampshade	7	6	■ ■	700–1000 +	1120–1600 +
Bohemian enamelled vase	7	7	■ ■	200–500	320–800
Burgun, Schverer & Co.					
cameo vase	8	8	■ ■ ■	350–1000 +	
Couper, J. & Sons					
'Clutha' vase (designed by C. Dresser)	8	8	■ ■	400–1000 +	640–1600 +
vase	8	7	■ ■	100–500	160–800
Daum Frères					
cameo vase	8	8	■	450–1000 +	720–1600 +
internally decorated vase	7	7	■	250–1000 +	400–1600 +
De Feure, G.					
vase	7	8	■ ■	100–300	160–480
pitcher	7	8	■ ■	100–300	160–480
De Vez					
cameo vase	8	8	■ ■	350–1000 +	560–1600 +
Despret, G.					
Pâte-de-verre head	8	7	■ ■ ■	300–900	480–1440
Fenton					
iridescent vase	7	6	■ ■	250–600	400–1000
Fostoria					
iridescent vase	7	6	■ ■	300–600	480–1000

Qualities on a scale 1-10 ■ Rare ■ ■ Very rare ■ ■ ■ Extremely rare

Object	Quality of manufacture	Quality of design and/or decoration	Rarity	Price (£)	Price ($)
Gallé, E.					
cameo vase	8	9	■	500–1000 +	800–1600 +
enamelled vase	7	9	■ ■	300–1000 +	480–1600 +
etched and enamelled vase	7	9	■ ■	400–1000 +	640–1600 +
Harrach					
iridescent vase	7	7	■ ■ ■	200–500	320–800
cameo vase	7	7	■ ■ ■	400–800	640–1280
Heckert, F.					
cameo vase	7	7	■ ■ ■	300–500	480–800
enamelled vase	7	7	■ ■ ■	400–800	640–1280
Honesdale					
cameo vase	7	7	■ ■ ■	250–750	400–1200
Kosta					
cameo vase	7	8	■ ■ ■	300–600	480–1000
Legras					
cameo vase	7	7	■ ■	300–900	480–1440
enamelled vase	7	7	■ ■	200–500	320–800
Lobmeyr, J. & L.					
drinking glass (designed by O. Prutscher)	8	9	■ ■ ■	900–1000 +	1440–1600 +
drinking glass	8	6	■ ■	30–60	48–96
Loetz					
iridescent vase	8	7	■ ■	500–1000 +	800–1600 +
iridescent vase (unsigned)	8	7	■	300–1000 +	480–1600 +
cameo vase	7	7	■ ■ ■	250–750	400–1200

Qualities on a scale 1-10 ■ Rare ■ ■ Very rare ■ ■ ■ Extremely rare

Object	Quality of manufacture	Quality of design and/or decoration	Rarity	Price (£)	Price ($)
Muller Frères					
cameo vase	8	8	■ ■	350–1000 +	560–1600 +
cut and enamelled vase	7	8	■ ■	300–800	480–1280
Nicolas, P.					
cameo vase	7	7	■ ■ ■	350–800	560–1280
Pallme König					
iridescent vase	8	7	■ ■ ■	300–1000	480–1600
Powell, J. & Sons					
vase (opalescent decoration)	8	7	■ ■	100–300	160–320
drinking glass	8	7	■ ■	60–120	96–192
Quezal					
iridescent vase	7	7	■ ■	300–600	480–1000
Reijmyre					
cameo vase	7	8	■ ■ ■	300–600	480–1000
Richard					
cameo vase	7	7	■ ■ ■	300–800	480–1280
Saint Louis					
'Arsall'/'D'Argental' cameo vase	7	7	■ ■ ■	300–600	480–1000
Stevens & Williams					
cameo vase	8	6	■ ■	300–1000 +	480–1600 +
Steuben					
'Aurene' iridescent vase	7	7	■ ■	400–1000 +	640–1600 +
cameo vase	7	7	■ ■ ■	250–750	400–1200

Qualities on a scale 1-10 ■ Rare ■ ■ Very rare ■ ■ ■ Extremely rare

Object	Quality of manufacture	Quality of design and/or decoration	Rarity	Price (£)	Price ($)
Theresienthaler					
drinking glass (designed by H. Christiansen)	8	8	■ ■ ■	200–400	320–640
Tiffany					
iridescent vase	8	7	■ ■	400–1000 +	640–1600 +
iridescent vase (unsigned)	8	7	■ ■ ■	300–900	480–1440
'Cypriote' iridescent vase	8	7	■ ■ ■	850–1000 +	1360–1600 +
iridescent wine glasses (6)	8	7	■ ■	400–800	640–1280
Union Glass Co.					
'Kew-Blas' iridescent vase	7	6	■ ■	250–750	400–1200
Val St Lambert					
cameo vase	8	8	■ ■ ■	350–1000 +	560–1600 +
Vallérystal					
cameo vase	7	7	■ ■ ■	300–600	480–1000
Vessière, C.					
cameo vase	7	7	■ ■ ■	350–800	560–1280
Webb, T., & Sons					
cameo vase	8	6	■ ■	300–1000 +	480–1600 +

Qualities on a scale 1-10 ■ Rare ■ ■ Very rare ■ ■ ■ Extremely rare

CHAPTER TWO

POTTERY AND PORCELAIN

Purmerend jardinière. Ursula, P16 Antiquarius, London. Price: £160.

For centuries potters in the West have tried to emulate the techniques of Oriental ceramics. During the period of Art Nouveau, the theme of inspiration from the East persisted, and European and American potters became obsessed with aspects of Chinese and Japanese ceramics which were previously unknown or almost unnoticed in the West.

One characteristic of Japanese pottery which fascinated Western artists during the second half of the nineteenth century was the painted decoration. Particularly innovative to Western eyes was the asymmetry of the designs, the intense naturalism of the drawing and the absence of any formal borders.

Rozenburg vase
Height: 39cm
Sold: Phillips, London, 19/6/86
Price: £187

DANISH PORCELAIN

The Royal Copenhagen Porcelain Company was one of the first European factories which produced porcelain decorated in the Japanese style. In 1884 the firm was taken over by the publicly-owned earthenware factory Aluminia, which was run by Philip Schou. The following year Schou appointed Arnold Emil Krog as artistic manager. Through visits to London and Paris, Krog became aware of Japanese art, and was particularly impressed by the pottery decoration he saw. 'There are no rules,' he commented, 'no styles, everything can be used: a volcano and a spider, a falling leaf and a Persian arabesque, everything is possible because it is used with complete artistic understanding of what is decorative. It is like a solo against a soft accompaniment – there is always a single patch of colour, a single motif which produces the effect.... For me it was a complete revelation.'

There had already been European pottery decorated with *japonaiseries*. In the 1860s Félix Bracquemond, in France, had designed a dinner service for the pottery and glassware entrepreneur François Eugène Rousseau, using decorative motifs inspired by the work of the Japanese graphic artist Hokusai. In England, several firms had manufactured ceramics decorated with designs, usually transfer-printed, borrowed from Japanese art. During the 1880s Albert Dammouse had painted Sèvres tableware with Japanese motifs, and some of Krog's early work is reminiscent of the French artist's decoration. But Krog and the decorators employed at the Copenhagen factory went beyond the efforts of china decorators in France and England, who had used the vocabulary of Japanese art without completely understanding the syntax. Rather than merely borrowing typical motifs such as fans, cranes and carp, the Danish artists sought their models in the Danish countryside but treated them in the Oriental manner. 'In Copenhagen as well as in Nancy,' wrote the French critic Roger Marx, comparing Arnold Krog to Emile Gallé, 'it is the surrounding countryside which acts as a source of inspiration and a guide; in other words, both M. Krog and M. Gallé maintain the fine principles of the Japanese, but in accordance with their own mentalities and their own climates.'

In 1889 Royal Copenhagen showed their new underglaze-painted porcelain at the Universal Exhibition in Paris. Within two weeks of the opening every piece was sold. The ware was greeted with widespread critical acclaim. What contemporaries found particularly agreeable about it was not only the Japanese style of decoration but also the softness of the colours and the elegance of the shapes. The pale shades of blue, pink, green and grey were the twilight colours so favoured at the end of the nineteenth century. The decoration seemed to loom out of the porcelain, rather than to have been painted on it. Sometimes the surface was gently broken by modelling in shallow relief. The 'Marguerite' tableware, designed by Krog, was decorated in pink and grey under the glaze; flowers appeared in barely visible relief and the handles were modelled as insects. In this range the coffee pot was given a handle in the form of a dragonfly and on the lid sits a bee for its knob.

Apart from Krog, the leading artists at the Royal Copenhagen factory were Gotfred Rode, Bertha Nathanielsen, Jenny Meyer, Marianne Host, Carl Mortensen and Carl Frederik Liisberg. A few Copenhagen vases were modelled as flowers, and others had pierced rims, shaped as flower heads. A wide range of figures was also manufactured; some of them remain in production today. Still popular is the *fin de siècle* eroticism of *The Rock and the Wave,*

Riessner, Stellmacher & Kessel 'Amphora' vase
Height: 63cm
Sold: Sotheby's, London, 16/5/86
Price: £660

a male and female nude group originally modelled by Professor Theodor Lundburg in 1897, and loosely based on Rodin's *The Kiss*. Copenhagen figures were painted in the same soft colours as the vases and tableware, but otherwise they have little to do with Art Nouveau. Typical subjects are animals, birds and rural figures, such as *Peasant Women Gossiping, Boy with Calf* and *Goose Girl*.

Following the Royal Copenhagen Porcelain Company's huge success at the Paris exhibition of 1889, the decorative style created by Krog and his team of artists was widely imitated. Some factories wooed decorators away from the factory. The Bing & Grondahl porcelain company, also situated in Copenhagen, soon recruited artists from Krog's studio; August F. Hallin worked for Royal Copenhagen for ten years before joining Bing & Grondahl in 1895, and Svend Hammershoi was employed by Royal Copenhagen from 1891 to 1894 and by Bing & Grondahl from 1898 to 1900. The artistic merit of Bing & Grondahl's porcelain rose appreciably in 1897 with the appointment that year of Jens Ferdinand Willumsen as art director at the firm. Willumsen had worked with Paul Gauguin at Pont-Aven and, since 1894, had had his own workshops and kilns. He had studied Middle Eastern bas-reliefs, and the work produced at Bing & Grondahl during his years there has a sculptural quality. Many vases were decorated in shallow relief, and openwork floral designs were a speciality of the factory. Among the artists who made them were Fanny Garde and Effie Hegermann-Lindencrone. Like Royal Copenhagen, the Bing & Grondahl factory also turned out a large number of figures.

Hasselt tile panel
106.4 × 60.8cm
Sold: Phillips, London, 19/6/86
Price: £550

THE INFLUENCE OF DANISH TECHNIQUES

Royal Copenhagen artists took their skills to other factories farther afield. Liisberg spent some time at St Petersburg during 1892, and the Imperial Porcelain Company in Russia began making a rather crude version of the Copenhagen ware. After nineteen years with Royal Copenhagen, the paintress Marianne Host applied for a position at the Meissen porcelain factory where she worked from 1906 to 1909. Meissen had already developed a passable imitation of the Copenhagen ware, and several of the firm's decorators, notably Otto Voigt and Rudolf Hentschel, had worked in the style from the late nineties. The Porsgrund porcelain factory in Norway also imitated Copenhagen, and so did the factory at Rörstrand, near Stockholm in Sweden. Alf Wallander designed for Rörstrand from 1895, and in 1900 he was appointed artistic director (he also designed for the Reijmyre and Kosta glassworks). The artists at Rörstrand specialized in openwork flower-shaped vases like those produced by Bing & Grondahl.

Minton 'Secessionist' vase
Height: 19cm
Ursula, P16 Antiquarius, London
Price: £58

As well as the factories which produced their own version of the Royal Copenhagen underglaze-painted porcelain, there were others which adopted the same range of muted colours: pale blue, soft green, pink, beige and grey. Arnold Krog and his chemists at Copenhagen appear to have created the palette which became the favoured colour scheme of the Art Nouveau style. Whether they helped to form popular taste, or whether they were quicker than most to sense the artistic current, has to remain an imponderable enigma, but the significance of the porcelain is indisputable. As Bernard Rackham, Keeper of Ceramics at the Victoria & Albert Museum, London, wrote in 1931: 'The importance of Mr Krog's achievement rests not only, perhaps not chiefly, in what has been produced by himself and his staff of fellow artists. It consists also in the impetus he gave to new endeavour in other quarters. Far beyond the boundaries of Denmark the effect is apparent.'

AMERICAN POTTERY

In America, the evolution of the Rookwood Pottery's decorative style ran parallel to developments at Royal Copenhagen. Maria Longworth Nichols, who established the firm at Cincinnati, Ohio, in 1880, had been impressed by the Japanese ceramics she had seen at the Philadelphia Exposition of 1876, as well as by French pottery painted with Japanese-inspired decorative designs which had been displayed at the same exhibition. In 1878 her husband, George Ward Nichols, had written a book called *Pottery, How it is Made, its Shape and Decoration* which contained six pages of 'Japanese Designs, Figures and Motifs' contributed by Mrs Nichols. From the beginning, Rookwood pottery was decorated with flowers, birds and landscapes treated in the Japanese manner. Among the decorators were Matthew Daly, Laura Fry and Albert Valentien; a Japanese-born artist, Kataro Shirayamadani, joined the staff in 1887. Another artist, W.P. McDonald, specialized in decoration featuring portraits of American Indian chiefs. His work is today probably the most keenly collected of all Rookwood wares. A colour scheme of brown, orange and yellow shades prevailed, and this ware was called Rookwood Standard. In 1889 it was well received when shown at the Universal Exhibition in Paris, where the Rookwood Pottery was awarded a gold medal.

The management at Rookwood were evidently impressed by the Royal Copenhagen exhibit which was awarded the Grand Prix at Paris in 1889. During the 1890s Rookwood introduced the 'Iris' and 'Cameo' lines which were coloured in the soft shades made popular by Royal Copenhagen. After the turn of the century Rookwood decorated much of its output with matt glazes.

In 1892 the paintress Laura Fry left Rookwood and joined the Lonhuda factory at Zanesville, Ohio, not far from Cincinnati. Other Rookwood artists followed her, and soon after, the pottery produced by Lonhuda was practically identical to Rookwood Standard. In 1895 the Lonhuda Pottery was purchased by S.A. Weller who changed the name of the ware to 'Louwelsa'.

Other imitations of Rookwood Standard were 'Rozanne Royale' manufactured by the Roseville Pottery, also situated at Zanesville, and 'Lo Moro' ware which was produced by the Zanesville Art Pottery.

POTTERY IN FRANCE

In France, pottery decoration developed from a more profound comprehension of Japanese ceramic art. This can be seen clearly in the work

Zsolnay lustre vase
Height: 14.25cm
Sold: Sotheby's, London, 19/12/86
Price: £572

Riessner, Stellmacher & Kessel 'Amphora' dish
Height: 46.5 cm
Sold: Sotheby's, London, 16/5/86
Price: £550

of Albert-Louis Dammouse who, having painted Sèvres and Limoges wares with Japanese motifs during the early 1880s, then began making his own porcelain and stoneware which he decorated in a much freer and more vital, although still essentially Oriental, style. Edmond Lachenal, who set up his own workshop in 1880 and at first decorated his pots in a Persian style, started in about 1890 to decorate his china with plants and insects treated in the Japanese manner. Subsequently he began using hydrofluoric acid to obtain matt surfaces which he usually decorated with more formal patterns of flowers arranged in the swirling arabesques of Art Nouveau. From the early eighties Emile Gallé began incorporating Japanese motifs such as fans, blossoms and seals in the otherwise neo-rococo ornament on his faience, but by 1890 he was producing vases decorated in the same style as his cameo glass.

Work which reflects the influence

of Oriental stoneware simply decorated with glaze effects was produced in a much smaller quantity in the West. Ironically, at the very time that Western potters began to imitate the glazes found on Japanese country pottery, examples of the original Chinese stoneware on which it was based were being unearthed from Sung dynasty burial grounds, disturbed for the construction of railways. At the turn of the century Sung pots started to reach the West in large numbers, but they were not to influence European and American potters until Art Nouveau had been defunct for some years.

Royal Copenhagen porcelain vase, decorated by Jenny Meyer
Height: 45.2cm
K. Barlow Ltd, London
Price: £980

During the 1880s, however, Siegfried Bing brought from Japan examples of Akahada and Shigaraki wares based on Sung pottery. Bing had come from Hamburg to Paris and had established a business dealing in Japanese antiquities and decorative arts. Among those who collected Japanese pottery was the sculptor Paul Jeanneney who occupied a studio in an artists' colony in Paris called the Cité Fleurie. In a nearby studio worked another sculptor, Jean Carriès, who became fascinated by the Japanese country stoneware in Jeanneney's collection. He had first seen examples at the 1878 Universal Exhibition in Paris; in Jeanneney's studio he could study the pottery at his leisure. In 1888 he decided that he wanted to make ceramics himself and he visited Cosne in the Nièvre, a region with an extensive rural pottery industry manufacturing stoneware. He settled in the neighbouring village of St Amand-en-Puisaye and, after much trial and error, began to make stoneware covered in wood-ash and felspathic glazes. The glazes on his works often drip down the side of the vessel and sometimes run into each other. The colours are mainly shades of brown, beige and blue; some pots are embellished with patches of gold, in imitation of the Japanese method of disguising flaws, and some with areas of a thick pink enamel.

In 1889 Carriès exhibited his first pots in Paris. Among the visitors to the show was the painter John Singer Sargent who recommended the pottery to his relative the Princesse de Scey-Montbéliard (the former Miss Winaretta Singer). The Princess owned the manuscript of Wagner's opera *Parsifal*, for which she decided to have a shrine built. The principal doorway, comprising several hundred panels each bearing a human mask, was to be executed in stoneware, and Carriès was entrusted with this commission. The project would never be completed but it was to occupy much of the little time left to Carriès. In 1895 he died of pleurisy and tuberculosis, aged thirty-nine. Other sculptural works in stoneware made by Carriès were *Head of a Baby*, *Head of a Faun* and some large grotesques, usually with the appearance of toads. None of Carriès' stoneware sculpture is available to the collector, but his vases appear on the market from time to time and are usually not too expensive.

Similarly priced, but generally a little cheaper, is the work of Carriès' followers. Soon after the potter's death Paul Jeanneney moved to St Amand-en-Puisaye and started potting himself. In 1902 he bought the Château de St Amand where he lived with his large collection of Oriental and European works of art. He made stoneware with decorative glazes derived from Far Eastern ceramics. He also cast in stoneware some sculptures by his friend Rodin, and others by Pierre-Félix Fix-Masseau (some of whose work was also cast in earthenware by Lachenal). Another of Carriès' friends and admirers, Georges Hœntschel, also sought to fill the gap left by the potter's death. Hœntschel ran an interior-decorating business, employing up to 300 craftsmen at a time. He decided to re-open Carriès' workshops and asked the painter, sculptor and potter Emile Grittel to collaborate with him. Hœntschel designed the ceramics which were then thrown, glazed and fired by Grittel, although they are marked with Hœntschel's monogram. They are generally more elaborate than Carriès' work, some of them being adorned with modelled flowers, plants or ribbons.

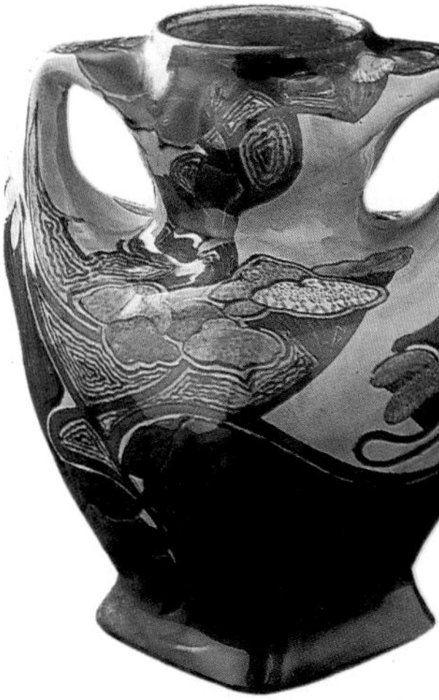

Rozenburg vase
Height: 24cm
Ursula, P16 Antiquarius, London
Price: £390

One of the local potters at St Amand-en-Puisaye who had helped Carriès when he had started his pottery was Armand Lion. He had become intrigued by the outsider's work and had started making Japanese-inspired stoneware himself. His son Eugène worked in the same style. Another potter, Jean Pointu, had settled at St Amand-en-Puisaye after studying various ceramic techniques in several pottery centres. He was in his late forties when Carriès came to the village, and under the sculptor's influence he too started to make stoneware in the Japanese manner; Léon Pointu, his son, potted in a similar style. Three other potters who were inspired by Carriès' example, and who worked for longer or shorter periods at St Amand-en-Puisaye, were William Lee (whose pots were hand-built, not thrown), Count Henri de Vallombreuse and the Swedish painter Count Nils Ivan Joakim de Barck. Examples of ceramics by these three artists are extremely rare and of rather lesser quality than those by Carriès and his immediate followers.

Around 1895 Joseph Mougin, a student from Nancy attending the Ecole des Beaux-Arts in Paris, saw an exhibition of Carriès' stoneware. He was impressed and decided to set up his own pottery. After some unsuccessful experiments and a period of study at Sèvres, Mougin and his brother Pierre established a workshop at Vaugirard where they made stoneware in the style of Japanese country pottery. They were encouraged by the Nancy artist Victor Prouvé, and at the turn of the century they moved back to their home town where they continued to make stoneware; some of their work was designed by Prouvé, Ernest Bussière and other Nancy artists.

GERMAN POTTERY

In Germany, Justus Brinckmann, the director of the Hamburg Museum of Arts and Crafts, started collecting Japanese pottery for the museum from the early 1880s, purchasing several pieces from Siegfried Bing's gallery in Paris. He lectured on Japanese ceramics, and Hermann Mutz, the owner of a pottery at Altona, was one of those who heard him. Like Carriès and his followers in France, Mutz, in partnership with his son Richard, began making stoneware in the style of Japanese country pottery. Richard Mutz was introduced by Brinckmann's assistant Richard Stettiner to the sculptor Ernst Barlach, and they collaborated on a stoneware plaque in low relief commemorating the Hamburg Museum's twenty-fifth anniversary. Barlach modelled the plaque with a portrait of Brinckmann in relief; Mount Fuji is in the background and Japanese wave motifs lap around its base.

CHINESE POTTERY AND ITS INFLUENCE

From the middle of the nineteenth century potters throughout Europe, and particularly in France, endeavoured to reproduce the rich red glaze found on some Chinese porcelain. The French novelist Gustave Flaubert has one of the characters in *Education Sentimentale* say: 'I'm so tired my dear fellow! It'll be the end of me.... I'm trying to find the copper-red of the Chinese potters.' Success came at about the same time to the Sèvres and Berlin porcelain factories. Not long afterwards, the problem was also conquered by the independent potter Ernest Chaplet working in Paris. When first exhibited in the mid-1880s, examples of Chaplet's *rouge flambé* porcelain and stoneware impressed Symbolist writers and painters. What was particularly fascinating to them were the mottling and veining of the glazes, the spots and streaks of green, violet, turquoise and black. Several other potters followed Chaplet's lead and made high-fired stoneware in the Art Nouveau style,

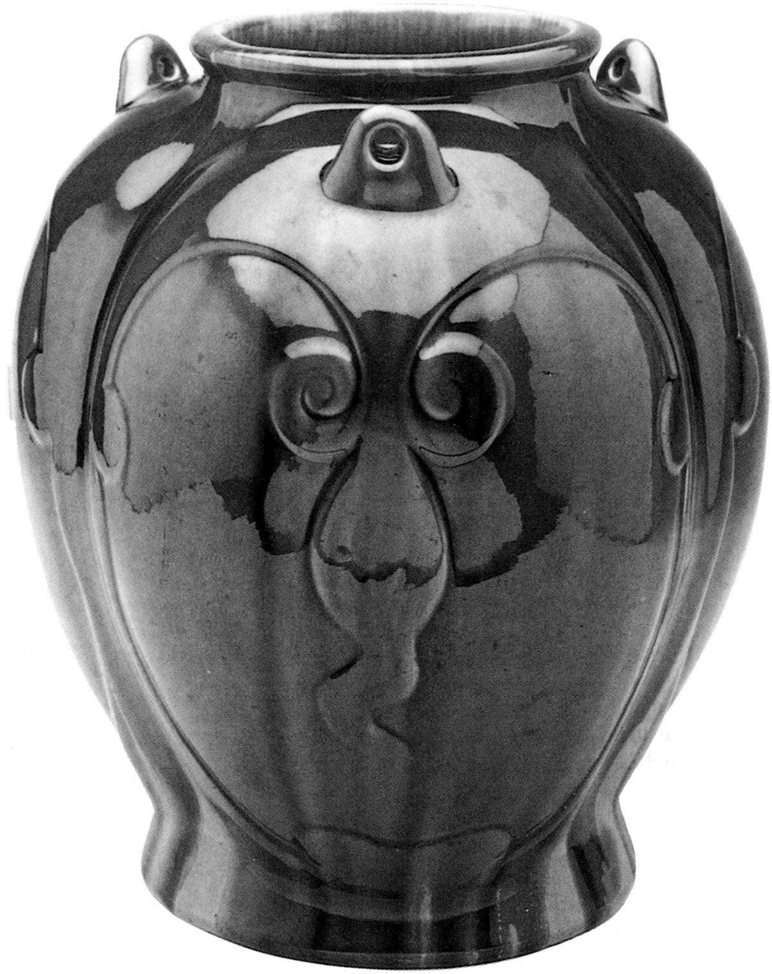

decorated with *flambé* glazes. Among them were Auguste Delaherche (who took over Chaplet's studio), Pierre-Adrien Dalpayrat (who invented *rouge Dalpayrat*, a deep liver-red glaze), Emile Decœur and Emile Lenoble (Chaplet's son-in-law). Alexandre Bigot in Paris and Emile Müller in Ivry ran workshops producing a wide range of *flambé*-glazed stoneware, including architectural as well as decorative ceramics and figures.

Linthorpe vase designed by Christopher Dresser
Height: 32cm
Sold: Bonham's, London, 5/12/86
Price: £550

Ernst Wahliss 'Serapis' porcelain vase
Height: 13.3cm
K. Barlow Ltd, London
Price: £250

In America Hugh Robertson began experimenting with copper-red glazes on stoneware at his Chelsea Keramic Art Works near Boston, Massachusetts, in 1884, and he achieved successful results four years later.

In England William Howson Taylor made *flambé*-glazed stoneware at his Ruskin Pottery near Birmingham, but the shapes of his pottery closely follow those of Chinese ceramics, and his work can hardly be called Art Nouveau. Bernard Moore, working at Stoke-on-Trent, Staffordshire, during the early years of this century, experimented successfully with copper-red glazes on stoneware and porcelain, and he helped Doulton's at Burslem, Staffordshire, to develop their 'Flambé' ware.

In Germany Jacob Julius Scharvogel, a co-founder of the United Workshops for Arts and Crafts in Munich, made stoneware decorated with high-temperature glazes in turquoise, red, olive green, black and rust. Later, he made stoneware designed by Walter Magnussen and Theodor Schmuz-Baudiss in elaborate shapes with relief decoration under a dark brown glaze. Meissen also made porcelain glazed with *rouge flambé*.

One of the offshoots of research into high-temperature glazes was the crystalline effect which was used to decorate stoneware or porcelain produced at Sèvres (where Taxile Doat made a speciality of it), Berlin, Meissen, Copenhagen, Rörstrand and Doulton's in Burslem.

LUSTRE POTTERY

Like the persistent endeavour to reproduce the Chinese red glaze, there were various attempts to revive the lustre decoration found on Middle Eastern pottery. William de Morgan, a friend of William Morris, was one of the first to successfully reproduce gold, platinum and copper lustre glazes. His work, however, belongs to the British Arts and Crafts Movement, and it is hardly Art Nouveau in style. Maw & Co. and Craven Dunhill, two factories in Shropshire, produced copper lustres decorated sometimes in a more Art Nouveau style. The artist Walter Crane designed for Maw & Co. and for Pilkington's in Lancashire which produced lustre pottery from 1904.

Clément Massier's workshops at Golfe-Juan in the south of France produced lustre pottery towards the end of the 1880s, under the artistic direction of the Symbolist painter Lucien Lévy-Dhurmer who decorated the ware with designs of flowers, peacock feathers, female figures and landscapes. Lustre-glazed vases modelled in the form of gourds by the Nancy artist Ernest Bussière were fired in the kilns of Keller & Guérin at Lunéville.

The Danish potter Herman Kahler, working at Naestved, made vases painted in lustre with designs of plants, and other vessels covered in multi-coloured lustre glazes, usually modelled with animals or birds.

Martin Brothers stoneware vase
Height: 5.2cm
Malcolm Haslam, London
Price: £250

The Zsolnay factory at Fünfkirchen in Hungary produced lustre pottery in an Art Nouveau style from the mid-1890s, some of it designed by the painter József Rippl-Rónay.

In America lustre pottery was made at S.A. Weller's factory in Zanesville, Ohio, under the supervision of Jacques Sicard who had previously worked for Massier, in France. The painter Theophilus A. Brouwer established the Middle Lane Pottery at East Hampton, New York, about 1893 and began experimenting with lustre glazes. His work is generally characterized by a pitted, iridescent surface.

SALT-GLAZED STONEWARE

Manufacturers of traditional salt-glazed stoneware in England and Germany also made forays into the Art Nouveau style. The art-pottery made by Doulton's at Lambeth in London was mostly decorated in a style associated with the Aesthetic Movement, but some artists worked successfully in the Art Nouveau idiom, particularly Mark V. Marshall, Eliza Simmance, Frank Butler and Frank C. Pope. At their Southall workshops, near London, the Martin brothers, two of whom had been employed at Doulton's, manufactured salt-glazed stoneware which was sometimes decorated in an Art Nouveau manner, for instance gourd-shaped vessels and vases decorated with sgraffito designs of fish.

In 1901 August Hanke became director of his family's pottery at Höhr-Grenzhausen, in the Westerwald, which produced the traditional salt-glazed stoneware of the region. He commissioned designs from Henry van de Velde and Peter Behrens for vessels which were then

Ernst Wahliss wall plaque
Height: 52.5cm
Sold: Phillips, London, 19/6/86
Price: £264

glazed in a wide range of colours, including *rouge flambé*. Reinhold Merkelbach, another factory in the same area, made salt-glazed stoneware jugs and steins to designs by Richard Riemerschmid, Charlotte Krause and Paul Wynand.

OTHER POTTERY STYLES

In the Netherlands, where the Delftware tradition had almost died in the face of cheap imported china from England and Germany during the first half of the nineteenth century, there was a revival of the ceramics industry during the 1890s, and much of the pottery produced was painted with Art Nouveau designs. The Rozenburg factory at The Hague made very thin china (marketed as 'Eggshell Porcelain') in exotic shapes with, for instance, elongated handles, flame-shaped finials, painted with flowers and birds on a white ground. Among the artists were J.J. Kok and S. Schellink. Pieces of Rozenburg 'eggshell' are always very expensive when in perfect condition, but ordinary Rozenburg earthenware, decorated with similar designs usually on a dark background, is cheaper and more plentiful. Several Dutch factories produced pottery decorated with painted designs of flowers, often formalized to such an extent that they appear to be abstract. Among the leading factories were Amphora, Amstelhoek, De Distel, Zuid-Holland and Purmerend (which became Haga in 1904). Designers who worked for one or more of the potteries were C.J. van der Hoef, C. Lanooij and Lambertus Nienhuis among others.

In England William Moorcroft, who later established his own factory at Cobridge, Staffordshire, started working for the Burslem firm of James Macintyre in 1897. He developed 'Florian Ware' which was painted with designs of flowers, foliage and peacock feathers, outlined in trailed slip. The ware was sold at Liberty's in London and Tiffany's in New York. In 1902 Mintons of Stoke-on-Trent, Staffordshire, introduced 'Secessionist' ware, designed by Louis Solon and John Wadsworth. The more or less formalized floral designs were covered in the polychrome glazes which Mintons had previously used for their 'Palissy' ware throughout most of the second half of the nineteenth century. Dr Christopher Dresser designed earthenware vessels in Japanese and South American Indian shapes for the Linthorpe Pottery near Middlesbrough and the firm of William Ault at Swadlincote, Staffordshire.

Apart from the American wares already described, Art Nouveau ceramics made in USA included the work of Artus van Briggle, formerly an artist with the Rookwood Pottery who, in 1901, set up his own workshop in Colorado. He made vases and plates moulded with relief decoration of flowers, animals and female figures, and covered with matt glazes. The Newcomb College Pottery, part of Tulane University in New Orleans, Louisiana, produced pottery with incised and painted decoration, and the Marblehead Pottery in Massachusetts manufactured vases with moulded, painted and incised designs of stylized plants or abstract, geometrical ornament. W.H. Grueby made pottery in an Art Nouveau style at Revere, Massachusetts. The shapes of his vessels were inspired by the ceramics of Auguste Delaherche, but his glazes, mostly matt, were original. A green matt glaze, delicately veined and mottled, giving the appearance of cucumber or watermelon rind, is particularly associated with Grueby's work. The Tiffany Studios, New York, produced a small quantity of earthenware vases in the forms of flowers. These are rare and always very expensive.

Art Nouveau ceramics made in the Austro-Hungarian empire fall into two contrasting categories. On the one hand, there were the factories producing elaborately decorated wares often moulded in the shapes of flowers and female figures; Zsolnay belongs in this group, together with the porcelain manufactured by the Royal Dux and Amphora factories in Bohemia (the latter not to be confused with the Dutch earthenware factory). On the other hand, there was the pottery and porcelain manufactured to designs by the artists of the Wiener Werkstätte, which was much more restrained both in form and decoration. The ceramics manufacturing and retailing firm of Wahliss in Vienna had a foot in both stylistic camps. In 1897 it took over the Amphora factory, but from 1911 it manufactured 'Serapis-Fayence' which was shaped and painted in a style strongly influenced by the Wiener Werkstätte.

Royal Dux vase
Height: 46cm
Sold: Phillips, London, 6/2/86
Price: £297

Object	Quality of manufacture	Quality of design and/or decoration	Rarity	Price (£)	Price ($)
Amphora					
vase	7	7	■ ■	50–250	80–400
Amstelhoek					
vase	7	7	■ ■	50–250	80–400
Bing & Grondahl					
porcelain vase	8	8	■ ■	250–750	400–1200
Carriès, J.					
stoneware vase	8	9	■ ■ ■	400–1000 +	640–1600 +
De Distel					
vase	7	7	■ ■	50–250	80–400
Delaherche, A.					
stoneware vase	8	8	■ ■	250–1000 +	400–1600 +
Doulton					
stoneware vase by F.C. Pope	8	7	■ ■	100–400	160–640
stoneware vase by F. Butler	8	7	■ ■	200–600	320–960
stoneware vase by E. Simmance	8	8	■ ■	250–750	400–1200
stoneware vase by M. Marshall	8	8	■ ■ ■	400–800	640–1280
'Flambé' vase	7	7	■	100–400	160–640
Gallé, E.					
figure of a cat	7	7	■ ■	750–1000 +	1200–1600 +
vase	7	8	■ ■ ■	400–800	640–1280
Goldscheider					
figure	7	7	■ ■	400–1000 +	640–1600 +

Qualities on a scale 1-10 ■ Rare ■ ■ Very rare ■ ■ ■ Extremely rare

Object	Quality of manufacture	Quality of design and/or decoration	Rarity	Price (£)	Price ($)
Grueby					
vase	8	8	■ ■	400–1000	640–1600
Lachenal, E.					
vase	8	8	■ ■	200–800	320–1280
Linthorpe					
vase	7	7	■	50–200	80–320
vase/jug (designed by C. Dresser)	7	9	■ ■	400–1000 +	640–1600 +
Macintyre, J. & Co					
'Florian' vase (designed by W. Moorcroft)	8	8	■ ■	200–700	320–1120
Martin Bros					
stoneware 'gourd' vase	8	8	■ ■	200–800	320–1280
stoneware vase (fish decoration)	8	8	■ ■	300–1000	480–1600
Massier, C.					
lustre vase	8	8	■ ■	400–800	640–1280
lustre plaque	8	8	■ ■	450–1000	720–1600
Maw & Co					
lustre vase	8	7	■ ■	100–400	160–640
lustre vase (designed by W. Crane)	8	9	■ ■ ■	500–1000	800–1600
Meissen					
porcelain vase	9	7	■ ■	400–1000	640–1600
porcelain figure	9	7	■ ■	300–900	480–1440

Qualities on a scale 1-10 ■ Rare ■ ■ Very rare ■ ■ ■ Extremely rare

Object	Quality of manufacture	Quality of design and/or decoration	Rarity	Price (£)	Price ($)
Minton					
'Secessionist' vase	7	7	■	40–120	64–192
'Secessionist' plaque	7	7	■ ■	100–250	160–400
'Secessionist' jardinière and stand	7	7	■ ■ ■	500–1000	800–1600
Newcomb College Pottery					
vase	7	8	■ ■	250–750	400–1200
Purmerend					
vase	7	7	■ ■	50–200	80–320
jardinière	7	7	■ ■ ■	120–240	192–384
Riessner, Stellmacher & Kessel					
'Amphora' vase	7	7	■ ■	400–700	640–1120
Rookwood					
vase	8	7	■ ■	400–1000 +	640–1600 +
Rorstrand					
porcelain vase	8	7	■ ■ ■	150–500	240–800
porcelain vase (glaze effects)	8	7	■ ■ ■	100–400	160–640
Royal Copenhagen					
porcelain vase	9	9	■ ■	300–1000	480–1600
porcelain figure	9	7	■ ■	250–750	400–1200
porcelain vase (glaze effects)	9	8	■ ■	250–500	400–800
Royal Dux					
figural vase	8	7	■ ■	250–500	400–800

Qualities on a scale 1-10 ■ Rare ■ ■ Very rare ■ ■ ■ Extremely rare

Object	Quality of manufacture	Quality of design and/or decoration	Rarity	Price (£)	Price ($)
Rozenburg					
vase	7	8	■ ■	150–450	240–720
'Eggshell' cup	9	8	■ ■ ■	750–1000 +	1200–1600 +
Sèvres					
porcelain vase	10	7	■ ■ ■	300–1000	480–1600
van Briggle, A.					
vase	7	8	■ ■	200–600	320–960
Wahliss, E.					
plaque	7	7	■ ■ ■	200–400	320–640
'Serapis' porcelain vase	8	8	■ ■ ■	250–750	400–1200
Wiener Keramik					
vase	7	8	■ ■ ■	200–800	320–1280
figure	7	8	■ ■ ■	200–600	320–1000
Zsolnay					
lustre vase	8	8	■ ■	350–700	560–1120
lustre vase (designed by J. Rippl-Ronay)	8	9	■ ■ ■	600–1000 +	960–1600 +
Zuid-Holland					
vase	7	7	■ ■	50–250	80–400

Qualities on a scale 1-10 ■ Rare ■ ■ Very rare ■ ■ ■ Extremely rare

CHAPTER THREE

DECORATIVE SCULPTURE

Bronze bowl by C. Kauba. Jeri Scott, P9/10 Antiquarius, London. Price: £490.

***Diana*, bronze bust by Georges van der Straeten**
Height: 66.5cm
Sold: Phillips, London, 19/6/86
Price: £781

How can there be Art Nouveau sculpture? If the phrase 'Art Nouveau' describes a style or tendency in the history of the applied arts, can it be correct to define any piece of sculpture as Art Nouveau? The answer is an emphatic affirmative. Yes, there was plenty of sculpture which was indisputably Art Nouveau. In fact, the question that should perhaps be asked is: was there any Art Nouveau which was not sculpture? Métro station entrances are as much sculpture as they are architecture; similarly, a corsage by René Lalique incorporating a dragonfly with a woman's body carved in chrysoprase may also be described as a piece of sculpture. In this context, it is not without significance that the Belgian architect Victor Horta used to model architectural details in plaster before they were wrought in stone; the Nancy designer Emile André also modelled pieces of his furniture in plaster before they were carved in wood.

THE BEGINNINGS OF ART NOUVEAU SCULPTURE

In 1892, George Frampton the English sculptor modelled in polychrome plaster a sculpture entitled *Mysteriarch*. It is a half-length female figure who stares straight ahead; the woman's face is framed by a disc behind her head and she wears a headdress formed from a bird's wings. On her breast hangs a pendant which incorporates the head of Medusa and a bat with its wings outspread. It could have been one of Lalique's creations, but it would be another three years before his jewellery appeared.

Mysteriarch is a perfect example of Art Nouveau sculpture for a number of reasons. First, there are visual elements which belong to this style, such as the pendant and the dynamic writhing of the figure's hair. Second, there are Symbolist allusions to the mystery of femininity; the circular disc suggests the cyclical nature of woman's existence, and Medusa and the bat represent the dangerous, predatory character of female lust. The title itself expresses how the *fin de siècle* male felt unable to fathom the female psyche and at once needed and dreaded to be subjugated by the woman. The psychological dimension of so much of Art Nouveau is quite patent in *Mysteriarch*.

A third indication that Frampton's sculpture is typically Art Nouveau lies in its material. European sculptors had done a volte face in the course of the nineteenth century. All the important sculptures of the first half of the century, by artists such as Canova, Thorwaldsen and Schadow, had been carved in marble, but during the second half sculptors turned to modelling in clay or plaster. 'A model finished in clay,' wrote the English sculptor Alfred Gilbert in 1888, 'is the last expression of the brain of its fashioner.... every touch conveys a meaning, and is an utterance of the soul of the artist.'

TECHNIQUES

The system had evolved whereby a sculptor would show a clay or plaster model at one of the annual official exhibitions; depending on the public's response and demand the model could then be cast in bronze any number of times or in a limited edition. It was further established that the most economical method of casting was the lost-wax process which reproduced every detail of the sculptor's model exactly, even when

Bronze table lamp
Height: 45cm
Sold: Bonham's, London, 27/6/86
Price: £275

it was deeply undercut. This meant that the elaborate finishing and polishing required after sand casting was eliminated. On the other hand, because casting by the lost-wax technique demanded high temperatures over relatively long periods, it was most profitably applied to small statues which could be cast in one complete piece.

In 1839 the Frenchman Achille Collas had patented a machine which could reproduce three-dimensional objects smaller; the apparatus had been extensively utilized by his partner, the bronze founder Ferdinand Barbedienne. Although Collas' machine was still used during the Art Nouveau period to reduce the size of statues for lost-wax casting in bronze, the two areas in which it proved particularly effective were medals and jewellery. For, by the turn of the century, sculptors were beginning to perceive that reducing the size of a statue was unsatisfactory because the statuette was itself a distinct art form. In 1903 a critic in the journal *Studio*, commenting on 'the special requirements of a statuette', declared: 'When considered in its relation to large statuary, it is found to have much in common with the essential difference of aim separating the short story from the novel.'

When *Mysteriarch* was shown at the 1894 exhibition of La Libre Esthétique in Brussels, the French critic Roger Marx hailed Frampton as 'a sculptor-decorator obsessed with dream and mysticism'. Marx was acknowledging a distinct role for the decorative, as opposed to the monumental, sculptor. In France a phrase such as *sculture de la vitrine* (showcase) was applied to statuettes made for the domestic interior; in England the writer Edmund Gosse campaigned constantly on behalf of 'Sculpture in the House', the title of an article he wrote in 1895 for the *Magazine of Art*.

If statuettes were to be admitted to the drawing-room, they would have to be a little more refined in appearance than the coarse, drab statuary kept out of doors. An advantage of plaster as a material for sculpture was that it could be self-coloured or painted after it had set. Bronze presented a greater problem, but a satisfactory answer was found in

French spelter lamp
Height: 54cm
Jeri Scott, P9/10 Antiquarius, London
Price: £450

patination (treating the surface with acids), a process which could produce a range of tones including several shades of brown, from honey to mahogany, dark green and glossy black. The development of techniques for obtaining patinas on bronze was probably instigated by an awareness in the West of the treatments that the Japanese applied to the alloys *shakudo* and *shibuichi* to give them highly decorative finishes. In Paris there were soon several craftsmen who specialized in the patination of bronzes: for instance, Jean Limet (whose workshop was close to the studio of the potter Jean Carriès in the Cité Fleurie, in Paris) treated bronzes by many of the leading French sculptors, including Rodin.

Gilding and silvering were widely used, either on the whole statuette or on parts of it. Sometimes gemstones were fixed on the surface of a sculpture, and often other materials with greater intrinsic value and more appeal to the eye were combined with the bronze. This led to such outrageous confections as Clovis Delacour's *Andromeda*: the woman's body was ivory, the rock to which she was chained was granite, the seaweed was bronze and the water was green onyx.

Spelter figure by L. Alliot
Height: 27.7cm
Ursula, P16 Antiquarius, London
Price: £230

BRONZE SCULPTURE

The demand for bronze statuettes grew steadily through the second half of the nineteenth century. By the mid-1880s there were some 25,000 men employed in the bronze foundries of Paris, and an increasing number of foundries were capable of casting by the lost-wax method. Technicians who understood the process migrated to France from Italy, where it had been used throughout the eighteenth century to provide gentlemen on the Grand Tour with bronze replicas of classical and Renaissance statuettes. By the turn of the century the leading foundries operating in Paris were Barbedienne, E. Colin & Co., Susse Frères, Thiébaut Frères, Hébrard, Joliet, Louchet, Siot-Décauville, Mario Biseglia and Valsuani. In London there was Alessandro Parlanti at Parsons Green and Young & Co. of Pimlico; at Thames Ditton there was A.B. Burton. At Frome, in

Pewter clock by A. Ranieri
Height: 57.5cm
Sold: Sotheby's, London, 16/5/86
Price: £374

Somerset, J.W. Singer & Sons built a new foundry equipped for both sand and lost-wax casting during the 1880s. In Berlin there was Buder & Wibrecht at Friedenau and the more important Gladenbeck foundry at Friedrickshagen. Brandstetter's and Leyrer's were the leading foundries in Munich, and in Vienna there was Westel Allgayer & Co. and Forster's.

The trade in bronze statuettes was international. In Hamburg, bronzes by French sculptors were cast by the Josef Kayser foundry for the Société des Bronzes de Paris, an agency set up for the distribution of French statuettes in Germany. In England, the gallery of Bellman & Ivey in Piccadilly, London, sold the work of French as well as English sculptors. At an exhibition there in 1894 bas-reliefs by Frampton were on show alongside a bronze statuette of St George by Emmanuel Frémiet.

Included in the Bellman & Ivey exhibition was a photograph frame modelled by the sculptor William Reynolds-Stephens. 'There is no feature more marked in the tendency of the day,' commented one critic, 'and certainly none more commendable, than the growing endeavour to adapt art to the beautifying of our domestic life.' Reynolds-Stephens sculpted several other useful items apart from the photograph frame. He also modelled a bon-bon dish with two kneeling female figures resting their backs against the receptacle; it was cast in either silver or bronze. Many British sculptors modelled similar items, and in France the practice was much more extensive. Domestic utensils of one sort or another were modelled with female figures, flowers or other motifs typical of Art Nouveau. Partly, at least, it was in response to William Morris's call for beauty in all objects of daily use. There was also probably an element of Japanese influence at work. Collectors and artists much admired Japanese bronze vessels, particularly incense-burners, which were generally adorned with animals, birds or plants, sometimes modelled in the round and sometimes in relief. In the West, sculptors created ink-wells, card-trays, knife-handles, finger plates, candlesticks, electric-light fittings and many other useful objects, which were cast in bronze and sold in large numbers.

Today, Art Nouveau sculptural utensils are generally cheaper than the statuettes. Multi-media figures (such as bronze with ivory, onyx, gemstones, crystal or another material) are usually too expensive for the collector on a restricted budget; so too are bronze statuettes by the more famous artists such as Alphonse Mucha or Alfred Gilbert. More accessible is the work of lesser known but highly accomplished sculptors. The price of a statuette by any of these will depend largely on how stylish it is. Bronze utility objects are quite often unsigned and therefore cheaper. Signatures on cast bronze are frequently difficult to decipher and it is worth keeping a list of the likely sculptors handy so that one can deduce a name from a limited sequence of letters.

Gilt bronze hand mirror by Maurice Bouval
Length: 33.25cm
Sold: Sotheby's, London, 16/5/86
Price: £990

Medals are the cheapest form of Art Nouveau decorative sculpture. They were very popular during *la belle époque*, and the concept of the art medal developed during this period. Medals were made for themselves, as beautiful objects, and not necessarily in commemoration of some event, or as portraits of dignitaries. Since the Renaissance, classical mythology or allegory had often been used as the subject matter of a medal's reverse side. Now, such themes were treated on both sides. There were medals with Symbolist subjects, sometimes presented in a very Art Nouveau style.

Many medallists at the turn of the century made most attractive, informal portraits of their parents, wives, children and close friends; genre subjects and even landscapes were treated on medals. The production of medals was aided by the Collas reducing machine, and more efficient presses meant that a greater amount of detail and relief could be obtained on the struck medal. Striking has always been a cheaper method of producing medals than casting. Most medals were made in bronze, but a limited number were gold or silver.

FRENCH SCULPTORS

By far the greatest amount of Art Nouveau decorative sculpture produced by any country was made in France. A brief survey of French

Bronze medal by F. Levillain
Diameter: 4.7cm
Malcolm Haslam, London
Price: £25

statuettes, sculptural utensils and medals of the period has to be highly selective, but here are the names of some sculptors whose work is more or less affordable today.

In 1895 a group of artists calling themselves 'Les Cinq' (The Five) was founded in Paris. The members were Tony Selmersheim (an architect), Etienne Moreau-Nélaton (a potter and son of Camille Moreau-Nélaton), and no less than three sculptors – Alexandre Charpentier, Félix Aubert and Jean Dampt. The next year they became 'Les Six' when they were joined by the architect Charles Plumet. In 1897, when another architect, Henri Sauvage, and another sculptor, Henri Nocq, became members, the group changed its name to 'L'Art dans Tout' (Art in Everything) which explained the philosophy behind it – no department of life should lack artistic beauty.

Alexandre Charpentier was a sculptor and medallist. In 1895 and 1899 he exhibited with La Libre Esthétique, and some medals he made indicate close connections with artistic circles in Brussels. He sculpted a medal for La Libre Esthétique itself and made a portrait medal of the Belgian group's founder and leading light, Octave Maus. It was probably through Maus, who was a lawyer, that Charpentier was asked to make a medal commemorating the general assembly of the Federation of Belgian Advocates in 1894. The artists of La Libre Esthétique were closely linked to the Arts and Crafts Movement in England, and it is likely that it was through the Brussels connection that the group round Charpentier in Paris adopted the artistic philosophy preached by William Morris.

Charpentier made several very attractive medals, including portraits of the writer and collector Edmond de Goncourt, the painter Camille Pissarro, and a fellow medallist François Coppée. The last was of a very irregular shape. During the second half of the nineteenth century medallists extended the range of shapes for medals to include rectangular and oval ones as well as the normal circular format, and occasionally they used irregular shapes, which were to become increasingly popular during the twentieth century. Apart from medals, Charpentier modelled low-reliefs and door furniture.

Henri Nocq also made portrait medals but he and Félix Aubert are best known for their lamps, mirror-frames and other useful objects in bronze. Jean Dampt produced a series of Symbolist sculptures including the marble *Volupté*, the ivory *Virginité* and the multi-media *The Fairy Mélusine and the Knight Ray-*

mondin. This group, a literary allusion derived from Symbolism, was made of steel and ivory with inset gold and diamonds. It would be quite beyond the reach of the average collector if it ever came on the market. But Dampt's medals offer some consolation; they also, sometimes, draw their subjects from Symbolist literature, and are infinitely cheaper. He also designed electric-light fittings in the form of flowers.

Maurice Bouval, a student of the sculptor Alexandre Falguière, designed a spectacular lamp in the form of cow parsley, with the flowers, made of glass, as a shade. Usually, however, Bouval's work incorporated the nude female figure, often in conjunction with plants. He made inkwells, covered boxes, pin-trays and other useful objects in bronze. The work of Louis Chalon is similar to Bouval's; his mantelshelf clocks and vases, bon-bon dishes and centrepieces usually featured the female figure emerging from a flower.

Charles Korschann, born at Brno in Moravia, studied in Vienna and Berlin before he arrived in Paris where he stayed from 1894 to 1906. There he made portrait busts (including one of Alphonse Mucha), statuettes and objects such as a combined lamp and ink-well in the form of a female figure, a *vide-poche* in the form of a female nude with butterfly wings, or a vase with panels of flowers in high relief.

Raoul Larche was one of the most prolific French sculptors working at the turn of the century. He produced a wide range of figures in a varied style which is not always strictly Art Nouveau, although his bronze of the American dancer Loïe Fuller, probably his *chef d'oeuvre*, is the epitome of the style. Several sculptors were inspired by Loïe Fuller's performance to make bronze statuettes which are often impressions rather than portraits. As well as Larche, Charles Louchet, François-Rupert Carabin, R. Jeandelle, Théodore Rivière and the German sculptor Bernhard Hoetger all made bronzes of Miss Fuller, and Pierre Roche made medals which depicted her. Portraits of Loïe Fuller are usually keenly fought over in the saleroom.

Bronze medal
by Jean-Auguste Dampt
Diameter: 6cm
Malcolm Haslam, London
Price: £40

Emmanuel Villanis made bronzes of female figures, usually head and shoulders, sometimes full length. Occasionally they are in the form of lampstands, but are more often purely decorative. He gave his females a tomboy appeal, at once young and knowing, which forces one to remember that child prostitution was rife in the capitals of Europe at the time. Some of Villanis' figures are enchained and have titles such as

Bronze figure by Albert Toft
Height: 33.5cm
Sold: Bonham's, London, 27/6/86
Price: £715

***Maid of Orleans*, bronze figure by Raoul Larche**
Height: 35.6cm
Sold: Christie's South Kensington, London, 25/7/86
Price: £600

Capture and *The Hostage* and were no doubt intended for a specialist clientèle. Georges Flamand catered for the same market with his partly gilt bronze vase entitled *Girl in Dungeon*, in which, however, the female nude is constrained by nothing stronger than clinging ivy. Flamand also made a pen-tray in the form of Leda and the Swan, and a combined

Bronze inkwell and pen tray by Gustav Gurschner
Width: 30cm
Sold: Phillips, London, 19/6/86
Price: £418

ink-well and pen-tray featuring three naiads cavorting in a lily pond. Auguste Ledru, Lalique's father-in-law, was a sculptor who made bronze reliefs, sometimes as trays, in the form of female nudes either in or near breaking waves. Lalique himself made a few medals, as did Carabin, the potter Jean-Michel Cazin and the painter Jean François Raffaeli; their bronze or silver medals are considerably cheaper than examples of their other work.

BRITISH SCULPTURE

Neither bronze statuettes nor useful objects in bronze were produced in England on anything like the scale they were in France. As a result, British decorative sculpture is rare, and, if often for that reason alone, expensive. The work of the best sculptors, such as Alfred Gilbert and George Frampton, tends to be beyond the means of the average collector, and what *can* be bought for a reasonable sum frequently lacks the style or quality of French sculpture. Some sculptors whose work can be found from time to time and has considerable merit, are Gilbert Bayes, Alfred Drury, Bertram Mackennal, Frederick Pomeroy and Albert Toft. Sculptured objects of use are, if anything, rarer than statuettes, but the work of William Reynolds-Stephens appears quite frequently and is usually stylish. He made a number of commemorative plaques which are not at all rare and ought to be inexpensive. Decorative caskets, light brackets and other objects were made by Esther Moore and Florence Steele, but their work is rare.

The best medallist working in England during the last quarter of the nineteenth century was the French artist Alphonse Legros, who made delightful portrait medals of, for example, Alfred Lord Tennyson, Thomas Carlyle and Charles Darwin. George Frampton and Gilbert Bayes also made commemorative medals which have considerable merit.

SCULPTURE IN GERMANY AND AUSTRIA

In Germany, a group of sculptors associated with the Artists' Colony at Darmstadt produced bronze statuettes and medals. Rudolf Bosselt, who lived at Darmstadt from 1899 to 1904, made a medal commemorating the Colony's first exhibition in 1901, and a fine portrait medal of Patriz Huber, another of the Darmstadt Colony artists. Bosselt also made a bronze statuette of Venus. Ludwig Habich lived in the Artists' Colony from 1900 to 1906, when he made bronze figures, including a statuette of Narcissus. Johannes Ködding also made some medals commemorating exhibitions and events at Darmstadt.

Some of the sculptors involved in the Vienna Secession made statuettes and functional objects in bronze. Of these, Gustav Gurschner is probably the best known. He produced candelabra, lamps and inkwells in the form of female figures with long flowing dresses, in a style tenuously linked to the work of C.R. Mackintosh and the other Glasgow designers. Gurschner's work is avidly collected and, over recent years, a considerable number of modern casts have appeared.

Maximilien Lenz was one of the first to resign from the official Artists' Association when the Secession started. He made bronze statuettes, among them *The Pearl*, the figure of a female nude holding a real pearl above her head. Georg Klimt, brother of the painter Gustav, who made the hammered bronze doors to Olbrich's Secession house, also produced several bronze statuettes and medals. The sculptor Emil Meier worked for a Vienna silversmith before turning to ceramic modelling, and made useful objects in silver, such as a hand-mirror decorated in low relief with a design incorporating highly stylized female figures in the manner of the Glasgow school. Wilhelm Wandschneider also made useful objects in bronze, such as a card-tray borne by a kneeling nude female.

In some provinces of the Austro-Hungarian empire were a number of interesting, avant-garde medallists. One of them, Stanislas Sucharda of Prague, made some medals with Symbolist themes, such as the cycle of seven plaquettes telling *The Story of the Beautiful Princess Liliane*. Another impressive plaquette by

Bronze bust by Emmanuel Villanis
Height: 25.6cm
Jeri Scott, P9/10 Antiquarius, London
Price: £500

Sucharda is his Symbolist *Spring* of 1904. Among his pupils was Bohumil Kafka who made medals in the Art Nouveau style, for example *Perfume of Roses*. He also made an irregularly shaped portrait medal of the influential patron of the arts in Prague, Dr Mánes. The Croatian medallist Robert Franges-Mihanovic worked in Zagreb making medals in a robust, dynamic style.

AMERICAN SCULPTURE

Sculpture in America during the last quarter of the nineteenth century was largely dominated by Augustus Saint Gaudens and Frederick MacMonnies, neither of whom generally worked in an Art Nouveau style, although MacMonnies did make a medal of *Niagara* showing an Indian brave in a canoe within a decorative border of fish. Daniel Chester French worked in a style related to Art Nouveau, but most of his sculpture was architectural, and was often carved in marble. Henry Linder was a silversmith who sculpted objects of use such as andirons, and Alfred Lenz, called 'the modern Cellini', was a jeweller who made small bronze figures in an Art Nouveau style. A good, though very late, example of his work is *The Dragonfly: Pavlova*, made in 1916 and inspired by the Russian ballerina. Elihu Vedder, perhaps the most remarkable precursor of Art Nouveau, designed a cast-iron fireback in 1882 known as *The Soul of the Sunflower*. It is one of four firebacks which Vedder is known to have designed in the 1880s. He was hoping to make a fortune from their sales, but they cost too much to manufacture and few were sold.

American spelter lamp
Height: 48cm
Jeri Scott, P9/10 Antiquarius, London
Price: £380

Object	Quality of manufacture	Quality of design and/or decoration	Rarity	Price (£)	Price ($)
Alliot, L.					
spelter figure	7	7	■ ■	200–300	320–480
Anon.					
bronze figural table lamp	7	6	■	300–500	480–800
spelter figural candelabra	7	6	■	250–400	400–640
spelter figure	7	7	■ ■	400–600	640–1000
spelter bust	7	7	■ ■	250–500	400–800
Aubert, F.					
bronze medal	8	7	■ ■	20–40	40–60
Bayes, G.					
bronze medal	8	8	■ ■	30–50	48–80
Bouval, M.					
gilt bronze figural hand mirror	9	9	■ ■ ■	900–1000 +	1440–1600 +
bronze figural tray	9	9	■ ■ ■	800–1000 +	1280–1600 +
Chalon, L.					
bronze figural vase	8	8	■ ■ ■	800–1000 +	1280–1600 +
Charpentier, A.					
bronze medal/plaquette	8	8	■ ■	100–500	160–800
Coppée, F.					
bronze medal	7	7	■ ■	20–40	40–60
Dampt, J.					
bronze medal	8	8	■ ■	25–40	45–60

Qualities on a scale 1-10 ■ Rare ■ ■ Very rare ■ ■ ■ Extremely rare

Object	Quality of manufacture	Quality of design and/or decoration	Rarity	Price (£)	Price ($)
Drury, A.					
bronze figure	8	8	■ ■ ■	600–1000 +	1000–1600 +
Frampton, G.					
bronze medal	7	8	■ ■	25–50	45–80
silver medal	7	8	■ ■ ■	50–200	80–320
Godet, H.					
bronze figure	8	7	■ ■ ■	500–900	800–1440
Granger, G.					
bronze medal	7	8	■ ■	20–40	40–60
Gurschner, G.					
bronze figural inkwell and pentray	8	7	■ ■	400–600	640–1000
bronze figural tray	8	8	■ ■	800–1000 +	1280–1600 +
Hoetger, B.					
bronze figure	8	8	■ ■ ■	800–1000 +	1280–1600 +
Jonchery, E.					
bronze figural candelabra	7	7	■ ■ ■	600–900	960–1440
bronzed metal figural frame	7	7	■ ■ ■	400–800	640–1280
Jouant, J.					
bronze figural inkwell	8	7	■ ■ ■	400–800	640–1280
Kauba, C.					
bronze figural bowl	8	8	■ ■ ■	400–600	640–1000
Korschann, C.					
bronze figural vase	8	8	■ ■ ■	700–1000 +	1120–1600 +

Qualities on a scale 1-10 ■ Rare ■ ■ Very rare ■ ■ ■ Extremely rare

Object	Quality of manufacture	Quality of design and/or decoration	Rarity	Price (£)	Price ($)
Lafleur, A.					
bronze medal	7	8	■ ■	20–40	40–60
Lalique, R.					
bronze medal	8	9	■ ■	150–500	240–800
Ledru, A.					
bronze relief	7	7	■ ■	400–800	640–1280
Levillain, F.					
bronze medal	8	6	■ ■	20–30	40–48
Larche, R.					
bronze figure	9	9	■ ■	500–1000 +	800–1600 +
Mackennal, B.					
bronze figure	8	8	■ ■ ■	600–1000 +	1000–1600 +
Meier, E.					
silver hand mirror	8	8	■ ■ ■	700–1000	1120–1600
Nocq, H.					
bronze medal	8	7	■ ■	20–40	40–60
Pomeroy, F.					
bronze figure	8	8	■ ■ ■	600–1000 +	1000–1600 +
Ramondeau, R.					
bronze figural vase	7	7	■ ■ ■	500–900	800–1440
bronze figural casket	7	7	■ ■ ■	400–800	840–1280
Ranieri, A.					
pewter figural clock	7	7	■ ■ ■	300–500	480–800

Qualities on a scale 1-10 ■ Rare ■ ■ Very rare ■ ■ ■ Extremely rare

Object	Quality of manufacture	Quality of design and/or decoration	Rarity	Price (£)	Price ($)
Reynolds-Stephens, W.					
bronze frame	7	7	■ ■ ■	300–600	480–1000
bronze commemorative plaque	7	7	■ ■	200–400	320–640
Savine, L.					
gilt bronze figural bowl	8	8	■ ■ ■	800–1000 +	1280–1600 +
Toft, A.					
bronze figure	8	8	■ ■ ■	700–1000 +	1120–1600 +
Vallgren, V.					
bronze figural vase	8	8	■ ■ ■	700–1000 +	1120–1600 +
Van der Straeten, G.					
bronze bust	7	7	■ ■	600–800	1000–1280
bronze figure	7	7	■ ■	700–900	1120–1440
Villanis, E.					
bronze bust	8	8	■ ■	500–1000 +	800–1600 +
Wandschneider, W.					
bronze figural bowl	8	8	■ ■ ■	600–1000 +	960–1600 +
Yencesse, O.					
bronze medal	7	8	■ ■	25–75	45–120
silver medal	7	8	■ ■	70–90	120–240

Qualities on a scale 1-10 ■ Rare ■ ■ Very rare ■ ■ ■ Extremely rare

CHAPTER FOUR

METALWORK

W.M.F. pewter wall plaque. Sold: Phillips, London, 19/6/86. Price: £660.

The development of the Art Nouveau style in silver and other metalwork is closely linked to the evolution of the style in jewellery design; often the firms or individuals designing and making jewellery would also produce decorative metalwork with the same technical and decorative characteristics. There are pieces of jewellery by Archibald Knox, for example, which show the same design references as some of his silverwork.

Nineteenth-century taste in silver and metalwork was on the whole revivalist or naturalist. Many of the pieces shown at the Great Exhibition in London in 1851 were interpretations of historical styles – medieval, Baroque or rococo – or else extravagantly decorated with plant or flower motifs, often reproduced with considerable botanical accuracy. They were seldom functional and always difficult to clean. The demand for decorative silver and metalwork far outstripped the supply of craftsman-made pieces. Consequently, cheap silver plate in (poor) imitation of the costly handmade pieces was churned out by the commercial firms, although no decorative metalwork was designed specifically for mass production.

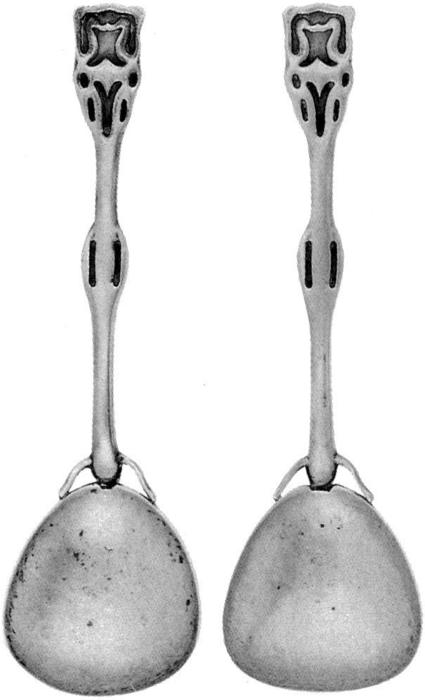

Pair of Connell silver and enamel spoons
Length: 17.5cm
Sold: Phillips, London, 25/9/86
Price: £110

ENGLISH METALWORK

The first new approaches to the design of silverware and metalwork appeared in the pieces made by the various Arts and Crafts groups in England. Although their work cannot be regarded as Art Nouveau their influence on the style as it developed in the nineties cannot be ignored. The Japanese taste began to manifest itself in their decorative metalwork in the early 1890s, in the work of designers such as Ashbee and his Guild of Handicraft artists. At the same time the Japanese emphasis on line and on surface pattern rather than three-dimensional decoration shows in the designs produced by students at the Birmingham School of Art which trained young designers and craftsmen for the industry.

One of the first commercial companies to manufacture pieces of a markedly different character to the revivalist or naturalist styles was Elkingtons, a Birmingham firm which employed Dr Christopher Dresser as a designer from 1875 to 1888. Dresser believed in the importance of designing for industrial production and Elkingtons was the first of several commercial companies for which he worked. His designs are almost without surface decoration, relying rather on an energetic use of line and silhouette to produce a visually satisfying object. Dresser was a botanist and many of his most successful designs were based on plant forms – not on a slavish imitation of flowers as decoration, but on the principles of growth and the natural articulation of one form with another.

Liberty & Co. of London were also marketing mass-produced silver and metalwork in the 1890s. This was sold (as was their jewellery) under the trade name 'Cymric', whereas the name 'Tudric' was given to their pewterware. Various designers worked

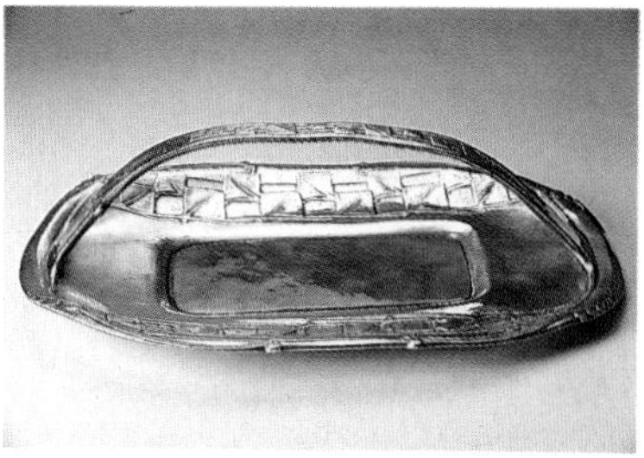

Liberty 'Tudric' pewter and enamel cake-tray
Length: 31cm
Galia Antiques, Q4/5 Antiquarius, London
Price: £140

Liberty 'Tudric' pewter box and cover
Height: 11.5cm
Ursula, P16 Antiquarius, London
Price: £285

for Liberty – Oliver Baker, Bernard Cuzner, Arthur Gaskin, Jesse M. King, Rex Silver and Archibald Knox. It was Knox who shaped the Liberty style, creating pieces in basically simple forms, decorated with tense interlacing lines derived ultimately from Celtic motifs. His decoration served to emphasize the construction of the object, whether it was a box, candlestick or picture frame; for instance, in his caskets designed at the turn of the century, the junctions of the feet and the body of the piece were emphasized with a knot of lines which develop into a bud shape, sometimes further accentuated with blue-green enamel.

The Cymric range included silver clocks, candlesticks, vases, cigarette cases, stud and jewel boxes, napkin rings, vases and picture frames, the bulk of them manufactured by the Birmingham firm of W.H. Haseler.

The first items of Liberty pewter appeared in 1901, also manufactured by Haseler. Much of it was designed by Knox who developed his Celtic theme further than in the Cymric range, with more direct reference to plant forms. Like his silverwork, he enriched the pewterware with blue enamels and turquoise studs. Other designers who contributed to the range used abalone shell as an inlay to create subtle blue-grey harmonies with the grey of the pewter. Pieces of Liberty pewter may carry different marks; some are stamped 'Tudric Pewter by Liberty & Co.', others are marked 'English Pewter' or 'Solkets'.

Liberty insisted on his designers working anonymously, so it is not easy to identify the originator of a design. However, it is sometimes possible because a piece may have appeared in an exhibition or have been illustrated in a magazine. The company also freely adapted the work of its designers and the design of pieces imported from the Continent. One result of this practice was the establishment of the 'Liberty Style' as a recognizable and coherent image which was widely publicized in England and on the Continent. The metalwork produced by Silver Studio and marketed under its own name bears the unmistakable stylistic stamp of Liberty; Rex Silver, the son of the company's founder, designed for Liberty and for Silver Studio. Alexander Fisher, like Knox, adapted Celtic motifs in his metalwork; however, he is better known for his enamelling, a technique which he learned in France and which he used to create pictures rather than to

Liberty 'Cymric' silver vase
Height: 19cm
Sold: Bonham's, London, 27/6/86
Price: £286

Hukin & Heath silver-plated pot designed by Christopher Dresser
Height: 22.4cm
Sold: Sotheby's, London, 16/5/86
Price: £990

make simple colour areas. His images have an affinity with those produced by the French Symbolist painters and his work is on the whole less concerned with the kind of structural emphasis which characterized Knox's work for Liberty.

The influence of the Liberty style was felt by other companies concerned with the manufacture of silver. Connell and Co. of London were manufacturing pieces at the turn of the century in the Liberty style while the established firm of Hutton and Sons Ltd. employed the young designer Kate Harris to bring an Art Nouveau style to their work.

In England, only a tiny handful of designers were interested in working for companies that made utilitarian objects. Dresser produced designs for Perry and Co. which were simple and functional, in keeping with his principles, and which were made in inexpensive materials – copper, brass and sometimes wood. William Arthur Smith Benson both designed and made lamps, light fittings, fire-screens, kettles, teapots, jugs and other domestic utensils. They were designed for mass production although he made them in his own workshops. His work in silver, copper and brass was virtually undecorated but manages to combine an awareness of function with a distinctive elegance of line.

METALWORK IN AMERICA

In America Art Nouveau metalwork was produced in two basic and quite distinct styles: a florid style based on the formalization of plant and other natural forms, which was inspired by French Art Nouveau; and a simpler style which had its roots in the Arts and Crafts Movement. Tiffany and Co. began making silver inspired by Japanese metalwork, with the same simplicity and clarity of form as that made by Elkingtons in England. In his own studios Louis Comfort Tiffany designed and produced enamelled copper and bronze vases, dishes and desk sets, experimenting to produce rich surfaces often with an iridescent finish. His work, like that of the French craftsman-enamellers from whom he learned, was extremely costly, because each piece was an individual work and involved a number of complex processes.

The Rhode Island firm of Gorham (the Gorham Manufacturing Co.) was the first company to introduce mass-produced silverware in America; its designs were fairly traditional until the late nineties when pieces mass produced in the Art Nouveau style began to appear in its range of tea and coffee sets, vases and bowls. These were made in curvilinear shapes with the handles and spouts

Perry & Co candlestick designed by Christopher Dresser
Height: 14.5cm
Sold: Phillips, London, 13/3/86
Price: £330

exaggerated into forms related to vines or water plants.

By the turn of the century several manufacturers of mass-produced silver and silver plate were adopting the Art Nouveau style, sometimes by simply grafting Art Nouveau forms onto existing patterns, sometimes by designing new pieces which are truly Art Nouveau in shape as well as in decorative motif. William B. Kerr and Co. of Newark and the Unger Brothers both made silverware in an exuberant style.

The Roycroft Community with its 'Copper Shop' outlets made metalwork in copper, brass and wrought iron; its work shows the influence of both the Arts and Crafts Movement and of the Wiener Werkstätte. The latter is not surprising since the Roycroft Copper Shop was in fact headed by Karl Kipp, a Viennese craftsman and designer. Although

Pewter vase
Height: 10.4cm
Ursula, P16 Antiquarius, London
Price: £49

Juventa pewter casket
Height: 13.5cm
Keiron and Sabina, N15/16 Antiquarius, London
Price: £148

Roycroft work was handmade, it was produced in large quantities and the workshop employed numbers of craftsmen to make up the designs of Kipp and other artists. Basically their work was sparsely decorated, relying on surface texture and strong shape for its impact. The elongated line of some Liberty and Werkstätte designs is characteristic of Roycroft metalwork, as is a use of organic shapes to highlight the junction of one element of the design with another. The Roycroft lamps designed by Dirk van Erp in copper with mica shades are particuarly interesting since, like the lamps of Benson, in England, they combine elegance of design with functional efficiency.

In Chicago the design of silverware and metalwork was much more influenced by the work of Frank Lloyd Wright than by either French or English prototypes. Clara Barck Welles sold silverware in strong, simple shapes with very little surface decoration through her Kalo Shops, and Robert R. Jarvie produced copperwork which shows the same attention to form and structure. In both cases the work may be described as Art Nouveau because of its emphasis on dynamic line and its lack of reference to traditional styles.

FRENCH DESIGNS

The Art Nouveau style in silver and metalwork in France was particularly imaginative and rich. Some of the most inventive and innovative craftsmen were working in France in the 1890s and jewellers and metalworkers producing small-scale objects of a basically luxurious nature were, next to the graphic designers, the most free to experiment. One of the techniques which was revived

French pewter candelabra
Height: 30.4cm
Ursula, P16 Antiquarius, London
Price (pair): £750

and extended by the French craftsman-designers was enamelling; some of the best enamelled work produced in France at the end of the nineties was done by Eugène Feuillâtre. His work was, and remains costly; Feuillâtre was not concerned with mass production and each of his pieces was unique. His influence was considerable; for example, the same technical concerns are evident in Tiffany's studio work.

Lucien Gaillard, who is better known as a jeweller, also made other forms of decorative metalwork. He was not concerned with enamelling but was rather more interested in the various Japanese techniques of patination and inlay as well as the use of

Tiffany bronze and glass inkwell
Diameter: 18cm
Sold: Phillips, London, 21/10/86
Price: £396

alloys to give his work a wider colour range without the application of surface colouring. As late as 1900, when he exhibited at the Universal Exhibition in Paris, his display contained little jewellery; his output consisted mainly of vases in various metals with rich patinations and inlays. Gaillard increased the range of metals used in decorative work simply by drawing attention to their various potentials in terms of colour or sheen. He used non-precious metals as frequently as he used gold or silver, the virtue of his pieces arising from their beauty as designs rather than from their intrinsic value.

The French word used to describe work made in non-precious metals is *dinanderie* and at the turn of the century several designers were working specifically in this discipline, which had been somewhat neglected elsewhere in Europe. Lucien Bonvallet made vases in repoussé copper (the repoussé technique involves hammering out the decorative motif in relief). Jean Dunand also used hammered copper, as well as other metals; he created vases in shapes based on natural forms – gourds and pumpkins – which were asymmetrical and strongly organic.

Of the large manufacturers, the firm of Cardeilhac produced some of the best pieces of mass-produced silverware and silver-gilt. Ernest Cardeilhac employed Lucien Bonvallet as a designer, who translated the motifs and shapes he was using in his own metalwork to forms which were suitable for mass production. Cardeilhac's products were less flamboyant than much of the Art Nouveau silverware in France; plant motifs were used with restraint and gener-

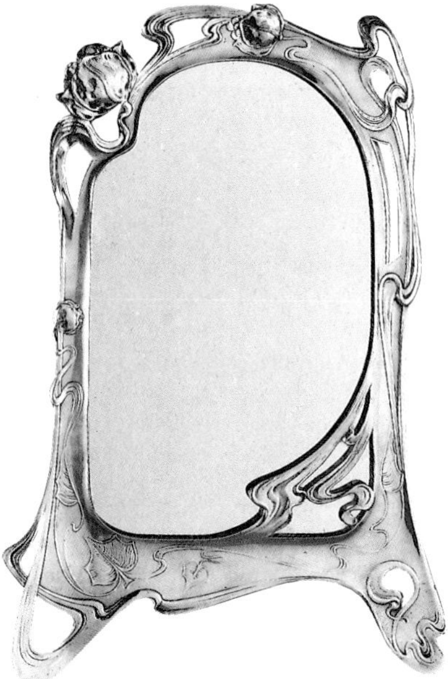

Silver-plated mirror frame
Height: 51cm
Sold: Sotheby's Arcade,
New York, 19/6/86
Price: $1045

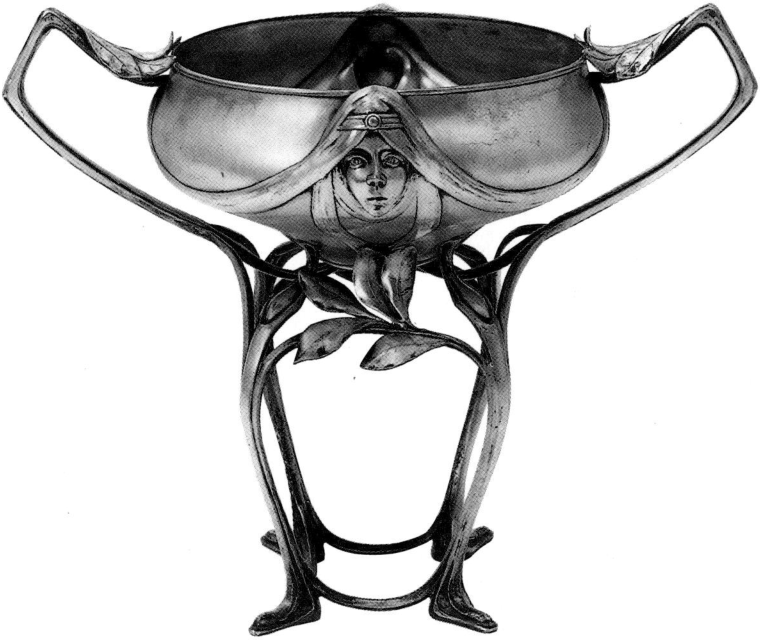

Silver-plated bowl by Hugo Leven
Height: 29.5cm
Sold: Sotheby's, London, 16/5/86
Price: £572

ally contrasted with areas of plain surface, and the handles of coffee or chocolate pots were made from carved wood or tinted ivory.

Siegfried Bing and Meier-Graefe sold the work of a number of silversmiths and metalworkers through their galleries La Maison de l'Art Nouveau and La Maison Moderne respectively. Paul Follot and Abel Landry made decorative silverware for La Maison Moderne as well as jewellery; Follot worked in a controlled, linear way with no reference to figurative images, whereas Landry who, like Follot, also designed furniture for Meier-Graefe, was more floral in his style. Maurice Dufrêne produced metal accessories for furniture for La Maison Moderne in the form of decorative hinges, handles and knobs, as well as larger pieces intended as door furniture. For La Maison de l'Art Nouveau, Georges de Feure made silverware and metalwork in a delicate and linear style which is clearly related to both his graphic work and his furniture design for Siegfried Bing.

Hector Guimard, the designer of the Paris Métro stations also designed metalwork on a smaller scale, including bronze picture frames and vases which relate to the exuberant organic forms and motifs in his architectural ironwork. At the turn of the century Edgar Brandt was

Urania pewter dish
Length: 30.3cm
Galia Antiques, Q4/5 Antiquarius, London
Price: £125

making decorative metalwork with organic and rhythmic patterns; both he and Emile Robert produced gates, balustrades and other pieces of decorative ironwork.

Unfortunately, firms who employed a skilled designer, as Cardeilhac and Falize did, were in the minority and there were few artists of Guimard's or Brandt's calibre who were prepared to make designs specifically for mass production. By the turn of the century the Art Nouveau style was not just acceptable to the general public, it was immensely popular, and as a direct result manufacturers who had held back from the new style in the nineties began to manufacture pieces which either copied the work of the pioneering craftsmen and designers or invented designs which exploited the most obvious characteristics of the style. The jeweller and critic Vever wrote disparagingly about this debasement of Art Nouveau, describing it as 'noodle style' because of the preponderance of writhing lines which appeared in imitative design. Vever blamed foreign designers and factories for the degradation of Art Nouveau, but in fact, as much bad work was being made in France as was coming from elsewhere and the florid style that was so typically French was perhaps more vulnerable to abuse than the more restrained and geometric developments taking place in Austria and Germany.

GERMAN AND AUSTRIAN METALWORK

Mass production and the active role

W.M.F. pewter basket
Height: 34cm
Keiron and Sabina, N15/16 Antiquarius, London
Price: £250

W.M.F. silver-plated, pewter-mounted decanter
Height: 38cm
Sold: Christie's South Kensington, London, 9/5/86
Price: £426

of the designer in industry were more important in Germany and Austria than elsewhere. Some of the best Art Nouveau metalwork to come from these countries was produced by commercial companies which made objects from the designs of members of the main German and Austrian Secessionist groups. Not all German Art Nouveau was in the restrained style, however; firms such as P. Kayser Sohne of Krefeld and the Württembergische Metallwarenfabrik (WMF) of Geislingen near Stuttgart made flamboyant pieces in pewter and nickel-silver, which were oddly shaped and decorated with writhing compositions of flowers and

Orivit pewter dish
Length: 27.1cm
Ursula, P16 Antiquarius, London
Price: £39

leaves. It was precisely these manufacturers and their designers, including Hugo Leven, the artistic director of Kayser Sohne, whom Vever blamed for the corruption of the style. He was, however, regarding it from an essentially French point of view; the flamboyant quality of WMF's work was not a corruption of the French style but an expression of the same kind of energy that appeared in the graphic works made by designers such as Eckmann and Sattler for the magazine *Jugend.* Mass-produced metalwork and silver was also made in an ornate style by the firms M.H. Wilkens & Sohne and Koch & Bergfeld, both of Bremen.

The style evolved by the German avant-garde designers, members of the Deutscher Werkbund and the Darmstadt artists' colony, was much

W.M.F. silver-plated mirror frame
Height: 35.5cm
Sold: Christie's South Kensington, London, 9/5/86
Price: £648

less flamboyant than the Art Nouveau produced by WMF or P. Kayser Sohne. Peter Behrens, Joseph Maria Olbrich and the Belgian Henry van de Velde designed in a manner which involved abstract rather than botanical forms. While still being organic rather than geometric, the shapes tended to be elongated and subtle in their use of the curving line, and ornament was confined to small areas rather than being allowed to cover whole surfaces. The firm of Metallwaren Fabrik Eduard Hueck, of Ludenschied, made pewter from the designs of Behrens, Olbrich and Albin Muller, which was characterized by its clean lines and elongated forms with decorative interlinked lines reminiscent of the Celtic-inspired ornament used by Knox in Britain. Behrens also designed silver-plated pieces for Wilkens & Sohne and several ranges of cutlery for M.J. Rückert of Mainz.

One of the largest mass manufacturers of metalwork, including silver, was P. Bruckmann & Sohne who manufactured the bulk of the designs produced by the Deutscher Werkbund in addition to employing Friedrich Adler and a number of other freelance artists to design pewter. Van de Velde's work was usually made by Hans and Wilhelm Muller at

Osiris pewter table lamp
Height: 43.5cm
Sold: Sotheby's, London, 16/5/86
Price: £682

Weimar; like Behrens and Olbrich, van de Velde worked in a style which was organic without being flamboyant; his pieces are compact, curving shapes, often finished with twisted finials or handles, in a different material from the body.

In Austria the Wiener Werkstätte designed an enormous range of metalwork, much of which was characterized by a use of abstract form which was more emphatically geometric than that used by Behrens or Olbrich. One of the most important influences on design of all kinds in Austria was that of the Glasgow architect and designer Charles Rennie Mackintosh whose work was well known in both Austria and Germany. The elongated geometric forms used by Mackintosh in his furniture designs and metalwork were developed by Josef Hoffmann, most particularly in the metal-mesh baskets made by the Werkstätte. Kolo Moser also used geometric form, but in a different way, designing vases and small items of silverware in absolutely simple shapes – cylinders and spheres – with no surface decoration except for lines of semi-precious stones.

The Wiener Werkstätte produced most of its own decorative metalwork and silver; the project had more than adequate financial backing from the banker Fritz Wärndorfer who, with Hoffmann and Moser, was able to select a highly skilled team of craftsmen to execute the designs of Dagobert Peche, Otto Prutscher, Eduard Wimmer and Carl Czeschka as well as Hoffmann and Moser. The great strength of Werkstätte design and production in the field of metalwork lay in the close relationship between the designers and the craftsmen responsible for realizing the ideas. Werkstätte metalwork was not mass produced in the same way as German designs of the same period were and it was made with a high degree of technical skill. As a result, little of it is available to the average collector today.

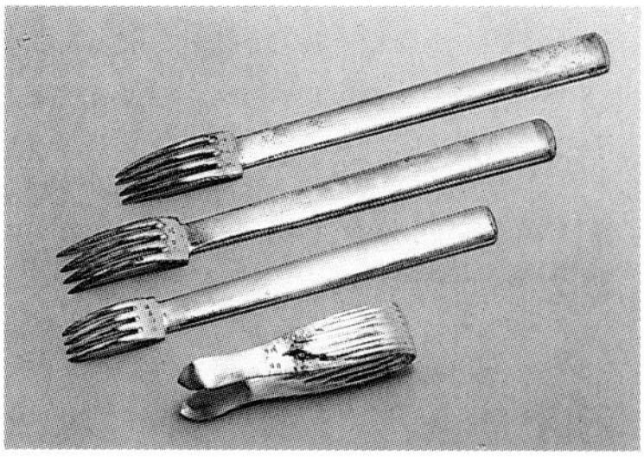

Silver-plated forks and silver sugar tongs by Josef Hoffmann
Length (longest fork): 21.3cm
Sold: Sotheby's, New York, 10/6/86
Price: $550

SCANDINAVIAN STYLES

Metalwork in the Art Nouveau style was produced in most countries in Europe; distinctive styles were developed in Scandinavia, particularly in Denmark where Georg Jensen evolved his own style out of international Art Nouveau, using forms which were heavier than those in French design, and less geometric than those developing in Germany and Austria. He made both silverware and pewterware in rounded shapes, with sculptural, formalized, natural motifs as decoration. Unlike most designers who were working at the turn of the century, Jensen barely changed his style, even after the First World War.

Object	Quality of manufacture	Quality of design and/or decoration	Rarity	Price (£)	Price ($)
Anon.					
silver-plated mirror frame	7	7	■	200–600	320–1000
pewter vase	5	6	■	30–60	48–96
pewter figural candelabra	6	7	■	300–500	480–800
Benham & Froud					
kettle and stand (designed by C. Dresser)	8	9	■ ■	300–500	480–800
Bruckmann & Sons					
silver coffee spoons (12, designed by A. Amberg)	8	7	■ ■ ■	350–500	560–800
Cardeilhac					
silver vase	9	8	■ ■	300–800	480–1280
silver bowl	9	8	■ ■	250–750	400–1200
Christofle					
silver vase	8	8	■ ■	200–400	320–640
silver box and cover	8	8	■ ■	250–500	400–800
Connell					
silver and enamel spoon	8	7	■ ■	50–150	80–240
silver bowl (designed by K. Harris)	8	8	■ ■ ■	700–1000 +	1120–1600 +
silver goblet	8	7	■ ■	250–500	400–800
Dufrène, M.					
pewter pen tray	8	9	■ ■ ■	300–600	480–900
Eisenloeffel, J.					
brass kettle on stand	7	8	■ ■	250–500	400–800

Qualities on a scale 1-10 ■ Rare ■ ■ Very rare ■ ■ ■ Extremely rare

Object	Quality of manufacture	Quality of design and/or decoration	Rarity	Price (£)	Price ($)
Gorham					
'Martelé' silver vase	8	7	■ ■ ■	500–1000 +	800–1600 +
copper (and other metals) teapot	8	8	■ ■	250–750	400–1200
Hoffmann, J.					
silver-plated cutlery (per item)	8	10	■ ■ ■	150–750	240–1200
Hueck, E.					
pewter plate (designed by J. Olbrich)	8	10	■ ■ ■	800–1000 +	1280–1600 +
Hukin & Heath					
silver plated pot and cover (designed by C. Dresser)	8	9	■ ■	800–1000 +	1280–1600 +
silver plated bowl	8	7	■ ■	150–300	240–480
Hutton, W. & Sons					
silver hand mirror	8	7	■ ■	200–400	320–640
silver and enamel frame	8	8	■ ■	300–600	480–1000
Isis					
pewter dish	7	7	■ ■	150–300	240–480
pewter candlestick	7	7	■ ■ ■	250–750	400–1200
Juventa					
pewter casket	6	7	■ ■ ■	120–200	192–320
Kayser, P. & Sons					
pewter inkwell and pen tray	7	7	■ ■	100–150	160–240
pewter figural vase	7	8	■ ■ ■	250–500	400–800
Klinkosch, J.					
silver centrepiece	9	7	■ ■ ■	800–1000 +	1280–1600 +

Qualities on a scale 1-10 ■ Rare ■ ■ Very rare ■ ■ ■ Extremely rare

Object	Quality of manufacture	Quality of design and/or decoration	Rarity	Price (£)	Price ($)
Leven, H.					
silver-plated bowl	7	8	■ ■ ■	500–750	800–1200
Liberty					
'Cymric' silver and enamel vase	7	8	■ ■	250–750	400–1200
'Cymric' silver mounted decanter	7	8	■ ■	200–400	320–640
'Cymric' silver and enamel spoons (6)	7	8	■ ■	400–600	640–1000
'Tudric' pewter box and cover	7	8	■ ■	250–350	400–560
'Tudric' pewter and enamel cake tray	7	8	■ ■	100–200	160–320
'Tudric' pewter mounted decanter	7	8	■ ■	100–250	160–400
'Tudric' pewter and 'Clutha' glass bowl	7	8	■ ■ ■	250–500	400–800
Mappin & Webb					
silver and enamel spoon	8	6	■ ■	50–100	80–160
Nieuwenhuis, T.					
brass desk set (8 pieces)	7	8	■ ■ ■	600–900	960–1440
Orivit					
pewter dish	7	7	■ ■	25–75	45–120
pewter vase	7	7	■ ■	50–100	80–160
pewter candlestick	7	7	■ ■	60–120	96–192
Osiris					
pewter dish	7	7	■ ■	50–100	80–160
pewter candelabra	7	7	■ ■ ■	250–500	400–800
pewter table lamp	7	7	■ ■ ■	500–750	800–1200

Qualities on a scale 1-10 ■ Rare ■ ■ Very rare ■ ■ ■ Extremely rare

Object	Quality of manufacture	Quality of design and/or decoration	Rarity	Price (£)	Price ($)
Perry & Co.					
candlestick (designed by C. Dresser)	7	9	■ ■	300–500	480–800
Ramsden & Carr					
silver tea-caddy and spoon	9	8	■ ■	800–1000 +	1280–1600 +
silver bowl	9	8	■ ■	500–1000 +	800–1600 +
Scheidt, G.					
enamelled cigarette case	8	7	■	200–400	320–640
box	8	7	■	300–600	480–960
Tiffany Studios					
bronze and glass inkwell	8	8	■ ■	350–450	560–720
bronze table lamp	8	8	■ ■ ■	800–1000 +	1280–1600 +
bronze and glass candlestick	8	8	■ ■ ■	500–750	800–1200
Urania					
pewter dish	8	8	■ ■ ■	100–150	160–240
W.M.F.					
pewter mounted decanter	6	7	■	250–500	400–800
silver-plated mirror frame	7	7	■ ■	500–750	800–1200
pewter basket	6	7	■ ■	200–400	320–640
pewter hand mirror	6	8	■ ■ ■	750–1000	1200–1600

Qualities on a scale 1-10 ■ Rare ■ ■ Very rare ■ ■ ■ Extremely rare

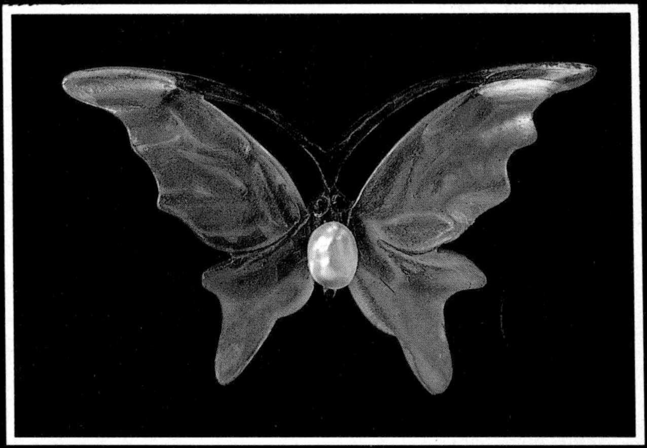

CHAPTER FIVE

JEWELLERY

Horn brooch. Purple Shop, London. Price: £78.

Jewellery design in the nineteenth century was characterized by two major trends – naturalism on the one hand and the revival of past design styles on the other. The naturalist style drew its forms from plants, and sometimes from animals or insects, which were painstakingly reproduced in precious materials. The revivalist trend plundered Gothic, Renaissance and classical forms with a greater or lesser degree of faithfulness. The jewellery in both styles was opulent; the people who bought it – the middle and upper classes of that time – liked evidence of 'value for money'. Obvious craftsmanship was appreciated (even if it involved only the ability to make exact copies), as was the use of precious stones, cut to display their brilliance to the best advantage. But Art Nouveau jewellery represents a reaction against the traditional treatment of materials and the accepted styles of design.

PRECIOUS VERSUS SEMI-PRECIOUS

There was an enormous demand for jewellery in the nineteenth century; the great craftsman-designers – the Castellani family in Italy, Giuliano in London and Léon Rouvenat in Paris – produced pieces which were costly, beautifully made and often fresh in their interpretation of historical or natural forms. But they represented only the smallest section of the jewellery industry. For every Castellani, Giuliano or Rouvenat there were dozens of commercial companies turning out designs which were endless re-interpretations of well-worn themes, substituting opulent materials for any real design merit. Pieces which had first been made in precious stones were often copied using the more brightly coloured semi-precious stones. In his novel *Against Nature* (1884), J.K. Huysmans makes slighting reference to the use of turquoise, 'the odious coral and the banal pearl', now that 'every small tradesman's wife wants a case of real jewels to keep in her lock-up wardrobe.'

With Art Nouveau came the idea that a piece of jewellery could be appreciated not because it was made from precious materials but because it was unique and exciting as a piece of design. Many of the Art Nouveau jewellers used materials which had little intrinsic value – horn or bone, for example – and semi-precious stones, which had been neglected by earlier nineteenth-century manufacturers because of their lack of 'display' value. Moonstones, for in-

Liberty 'Cymric' silver and enamel buttons
Diameter: 2.5cm
Sold: Phillips, London, 21/10/86
Price: £99

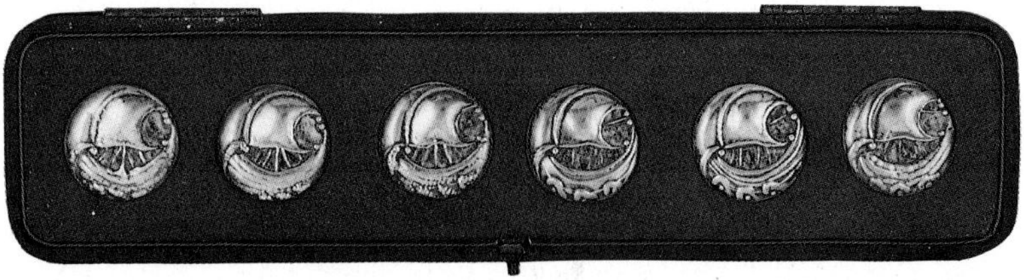

Liberty silver, enamel and turquoise pendant
Height: 5cm
Sold: Phillips, London, 21/10/86
Price: £165

MATERIALS AND TECHNIQUES

Enamelling had been revived in the earlier part of the century when Gothic jewellery became fashionable once more. The technique that became most widely used was cloisonné, in which the design is 'drawn' with metal wires onto a metal ground and then filled in with a mixture of powdered glass, which is heated to liquefy the powder and fuse it to the metal. *Plique à jour* is similar to cloisonné, with one impor-

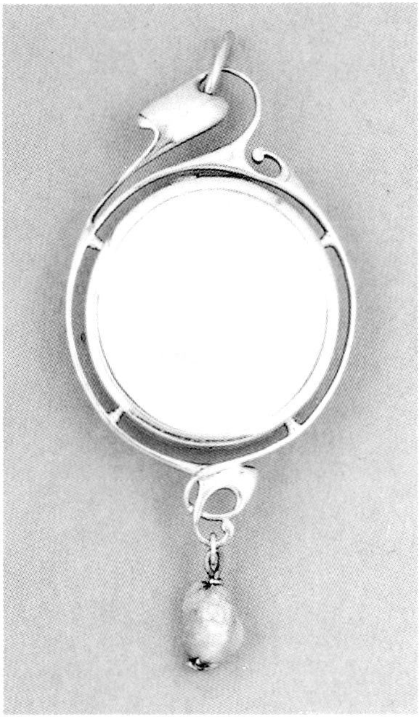

Murrle Bennett gold, mother-of-pearl and pearl pendant
Height: 5.5cm
Sold: Phillips, London, 21/10/86
Price: £220

stance, were barely used until the 1890s. Only then were they appreciated for their liquid quality and irregular shape. In a similar way the baroque pearl was an ideal jewel for the Art Nouveau designer because of its manifestly organic shape.

Silver, marcasite, pearl and *plique-à-jour* enamel pendant
Height: 6cm
Purple Shop, London
Price: £485

tant difference – in *plique à jour* there is no metal ground, so the finished piece resembles a stained glass window with transparent or translucent areas of enamel held by metal lines. Traditionally, *plique à jour* was made by outlining the design and filling it in on a background of metal to which the glass would not fuse and which could be removed after the process was complete. An alternative was to construct it on copper which could be dissolved with acid, which did not affect either the enamel or the gold of the design. Champlevé involves enamelling onto a metal base which has been moulded or carved to make hollows. These hollows are filled with layers of enamel as the work is created. The depth of enamel in champlevé allows layers of different colours to be applied which gives dimension and richness to the surface; in addition, coloured foils or flecks of gold can be embedded in the layers.

Glass was used in a variety of ways but not as a substitute for stones; it was moulded, frosted and coloured and used to contrast with opaque materials. It was set into pendants, or into brooches as decorative plaques, or formed into the female face that was a standard image in Art Nouveau jewellery.

Carved horn, bone and ivory were popular with designers everywhere in Europe. Being organic materials they were particularly appropriate for the expression of natural shapes. Mother-of-pearl was used for its iridiscent surface; opals were favoured for the same reason. A huge range of transparent and opaque semi-precious stones were carved or polished to create tiny sculptures for jewellery. Faceted stones cut in the traditional way to give maximum brilliance, were very seldom used; the geometric quality of such stones made them inappropriate for jewellery which was organic in its design, and the refracted glitter produced by faceting was at odds with the surface unity of the best of Art Nouveau jewellery designs.

INFLUENCES

Several strands of influence feed into Art Nouveau; the naturalism of the early nineteenth century was certainly important, although the designers of the 1890s were no longer concerned with the simple reproduction of natural forms. A growing appreciation of the stylized plant and animal shapes in Japanese art was an important factor in the translation of European naturalism into Art Nouveau. It is significant that both Arthur Liberty in London and Siegfried Bing in Paris, two of the most important disseminators of Art Nouveau design, were involved in importing and marketing items of Japanese art.

The English Arts and Crafts movement influenced all aspects of the applied arts at the turn of the century, impressing on them a spirit of reform and a rejection of unthinking eclecticism and inappropriate naturalism. The movement produced some jewellery that could be termed early Art Nouveau, which was influential in Germany and Austria.

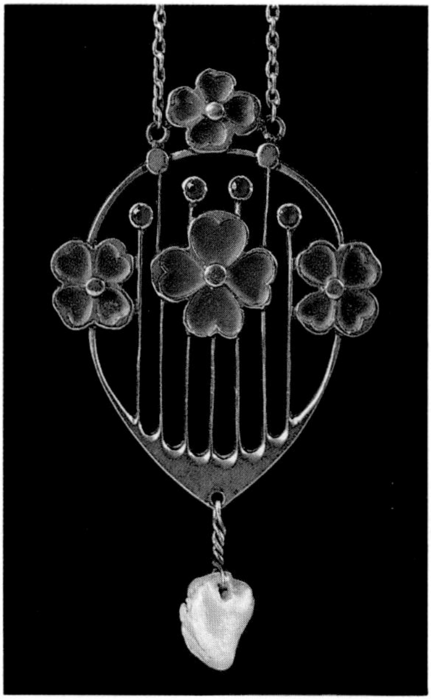

Silver gilt, ruby, pearl and *plique-à-jour* enamel pendant
Height: 5.9cm
Purple Shop, London
Price: £265

ENGLISH JEWELLERS

A large team of designers worked for Liberty; some were commissioned as a result of the competitions run by the magazine *Studio*, in which artists were invited to submit designs for jewellery, among other things. Liberty bought the winning designs and produced them for sale in his London shop or at the Paris branch in the rue de l'Opéra. However, it was company policy that designers did not work under their own names. Archibald Knox for example, one of the most innovative of Liberty's team, was not credited as an individual designer; his pieces were marketed as the Cymric range. It was Knox who first adapted Celtic motifs; he reinterpreted their abstract interlaced forms in silver and gold with inlaid mother-of-pearl, turquoise or enamel, and stressed their curving lines so that they became more explicitly rhythmic, expanding into controlled 'whiplash' lines. Rex Silver, Bernard Cuzner, Arthur Gaskin and Jessie M. King also made designs for the Cymric range; like Knox, their work was not individually credited.

It was essential to Liberty that the jewellery he commissioned could be produced commercially. With this idea in mind, in 1902 Liberty merged with the Birmingham firm of W.H. Haseler, which manufactured most of the Cymric pieces. (Even so, Haseler continued to produce jewellery under its own name, most of which was

Charles Horner silver and mother-of-pearl pendant
Height: 3cm
Sold: Phillips, London, 13/3/86
Price: £99

almost identical to Liberty's.) Other companies associated with Liberty were Connell & Co. and Murrle Bennett, both of which made and marketed jewellery in the new style. Both were influenced by the Celtic motifs used by Knox, some of whose designs were made by Murrle Bennett for sale through Liberty. The relationship between Liberty's designers and the manufacturing companies is sometimes confusing. On the whole the work of designers first commissioned by Liberty was sold only through the shop irrespective of the manufacturer but there are exceptions: Jessie M. King, for example, designed some

Diamond and pearl pendant
Height: 3.5cm
Sold: Phillips, London, 21/10/86
Price: £319

delicate, very linear, pieces for Murrle Bennett which were sold under that company's name. In addition to trading with Liberty, Murrle Bennett also imported German pieces and manufactured jewellery from German designs, thereby further contributing to the already fertile interchange of ideas between England and Germany.

The Charles Horner factory in Halifax produced some of the best truly mass-produced jewellery at the turn of the century. All its output was machinemade and low priced. Most of the designs for the firm were made by Charles Horner, the son of the founder of the company, and were clearly influenced by Liberty. Horner simplified the Cymric range, translating it into silver and enamel and into shapes suitable for the pendants, brooches and hatpins for which the company was best known.

Of the independent designers working in Britain Frederick Partridge and his colleague Ella Naper are worth mentioning. Both worked in horn, producing decorative combs embellished with semi-precious stones; their work is more florid than anything made by Liberty at the time and demonstrates the influence of French Art Nouveau in Britain.

FRENCH DESIGNERS

Just as Liberty & Co. was a focal point for new jewellery design in Britain, so were Siegfried Bing's La Maison de l'Art Nouveau and Meier-

Graefe's La Maison Moderne for the new style in France. Bing commissioned and encouraged artists working in all the design disciplines and it was for his shop that Edward Colonna designed some of his best jewellery between 1898 and 1903. His work developed from an interpretation of plant forms into designs of almost purely abstract curving and interlacing lines enclosing blisters of enamel, coral or pearl. La Maison Moderne commissioned the graphic designer Manuel Orazi, as well as Maurice Dufrêne and Paul Follot to design jewellery for its gallery. Between them the two shops expressed the range of styles covered by the term 'Art Nouveau'; Orazi's designs were the most bizarre, based on animated vegetable and animal forms with a strong element of fantasy, and at the other extreme, Follot made pieces which were simple and almost angular, relying on abstract forms for their effect.

It is impossible to talk about Art Nouveau jewellery in France without discussing Lalique, his considerable influence and the innovations he made in technique. Originally, Lalique sold his designs through established companies such as Louis Aucoc, for whom he worked early in his career, but in 1885 he acquired his own workshop from Jules Destape who had also bought Lalique's designs on a regular basis. Once established, and with his own means of production, Lalique was able to develop his characteristic style and to experiment with enamelling, glass and organic materials such as horn, bone and ivory.

By the beginning of the 1890s he had produced the first Art Nouveau jewels which incorporated the motif of the female figure with plant forms and fantastic insects, expressed in gold, enamel, glass, ivory and a range of semi-precious stones. Although there was always a strong element of fantasy in his work it was restrained by his sense of discipline and rhythm. His importance was recognized at the Universal Exhibition in Paris in 1900. There, his pavilion received almost hysterical attention from the public and critics and Lalique was awarded the Grand Prix and the Légion d'Honneur. In the following years he exhibited in Turin, Berlin, St Louis and London. In 1908 he acquired a glass factory near Paris and

Silver, ruby and pearl pendant
Height: 5cm
Sold: Phillips, London, 21/10/86
Price: £165

began to incorporate more glass into his work, eventually producing pieces which were simple glass plaques with no embellishment other than a moulded or carved design.

Many of the typical motifs of Art Nouveau can be credited to Lalique. He was the first Art Nouveau jeweller to use the female nude in his designs; the fantastic hybrid human and insect creatures which appeared first in graphic design were successfully translated by Lalique into three dimensions. It was he who made the most interesting developments in enamelling, evolving methods for layering in different colours and embedding metallic foils and flakes into the enamel surface. To extend the use of *plique à jour*, which was too fragile to be employed for anything other than small areas, Lalique evolved a method of carving the areas to be filled with enamel from one sheet of gold rather than constructing them individually out of wire.

Silver, pearl and enamel pendant
Height: 4.8cm
Purple Shop, London
Price: £78

Like all innovators, Lalique was copied by innumerable unnamed designers working for the commercial companies. Some of his motifs were repeated *ad nauseam*; the female profile with surrounding masses of serpentine hair was a particular favourite, winged women another. Some of these copies are quite creditable, made in good-quality materials; some, however, are crude, clumsy in workmanship and made from cheap metals. It is significant that it was Lalique's designs that were most imitated in the Art Nouveau jewellery revival of the late 1960s. Sadly, though, the lasting reputation of Lalique, and the inventiveness and high quality of his work make most of his jewellery inaccessible to the ordinary collector.

The Vever family enjoyed a reputation almost as great as Lalique's, as did the firm of Fouquet. Paul and Henri Vever commissioned designs from Eugène Grasset who was already established as a respected graphic designer, and Georges Fouquet employed a pupil of Grasset's, Charles Desrosiers. In both cases the relationship was that between a company with a high standard of craftsmanship and an innovative designer, and was fruitful with a lasting effect that went beyond the actual period of collaboration. Grasset translated into three-dimensional terms the themes and motifs that he had already developed in his posters: stylized female figures set in landscapes expressed in strong rhythmic lines.

Fouquet also commissioned work from Alphonse Mucha who decorated Fouquet's new shop in the rue Royale

Murrle Bennett silver and turquoise pendant
Height: 4cm
Purple Shop, London
Price: £98

in Paris and produced a series of striking designs over the two years of their collaboration. Much of Mucha's work was theatrical, in fact he designed stage jewellery for Sarah Bernhardt. He evolved a style which incorporated painted miniatures executed in the same linear technique that he used in his poster designs. Some of his pieces for Fouquet are tiny paintings set in gold frames, the lines of which echo the flow of drapery or hair in the central image. His influence can be seen in the work of René Péan who also combined painted images with jewels.

Lucien Gaillard was, of all the great French craftsman-jewellers, the most influenced by Japanese design. Before turning his attention to the manufacture of jewellery he had imported craftsmen from Japan to work in his company which, prior to 1900, was mainly concerned with the production of small-scale metalwork. His jewellery was rather simpler than that of Lalique, Fouquet or Vever; he used less enamelling, but relied on patinated metal instead to achieve rich surfaces which were then further enlivened with coloured stones and small areas of enamel. There are also fewer bizarre and fantastic elements in his work; he tended to use plant forms in a straightforwardly stylized manner which owed something to Japanese art, expressing them in organic materials – horn and ivory for petals, or insect wings enriched with opals and pearls which he loved for their luminous quality.

Many enamellists were employed by manufacturers specifically to design and produce fine pieces which required a high degree of skill and specialization. Eugène Feuillâtre worked for Lalique before setting up his own workshop and his own designs bear evidence of Lalique's influence. Etienne Tourette, Louis Houillon and André-Fernand Thesmar all made enamelled pieces for various manufacturers including Fouquet, while Paul Grandhomme and Alfred Garnier worked together for Grandhomme's firm.

Of the established jewellery houses – Boucheron, Chaumet and Cartier – only Cartier really adopted the Art Nouveau techniques. Boucheron and Chaumet commissioned some pieces from designers such as Edmond Henri Becker, but they were mainly concerned with the production of costly and elaborate pieces which paid only passing attention to the real developments of Art Nouveau. Cartier commissioned works from the Belgian Philippe Wolfers and the Frenchman Georges Le Turcq. These works were somewhat less costly than their traditional range and are truly Art Nouveau in that Wolfers and Le Turcq used enamel and semi-precious stones as well as some of the natural substances, like horn. La Maison Aucoc, which had bought designs from Lalique at the beginning of his career, also commissioned works from Edmond Henri Becker.

Another jewellery firm which created a sensation at the 1900 Exhibition was the Paris company of Piel Frères. Its work was fashionable but made from inexpensive materials – silver and gilt rather than gold – and it developed a technique for enamelling onto copper, a difficult process because of the low melting point of the material. Piel Frères was one of the first jewellery firms to use plastic, in this case celluloid, as a substitute for ivory and horn. Alexandre Piel, the head of the firm, employed Gabriel Stalin as his artistic director. The result of this collaboration was a range of jewellery that was inexpensive but still very beautiful; Stalin designed specifically for the materials he had rather than producing elaborate pieces which were better suited to precious materials and hand-crafting.

Unger Brothers brooch
Width: 4.5cm
Sold: Phillips, London, 21/10/86
Price: £99

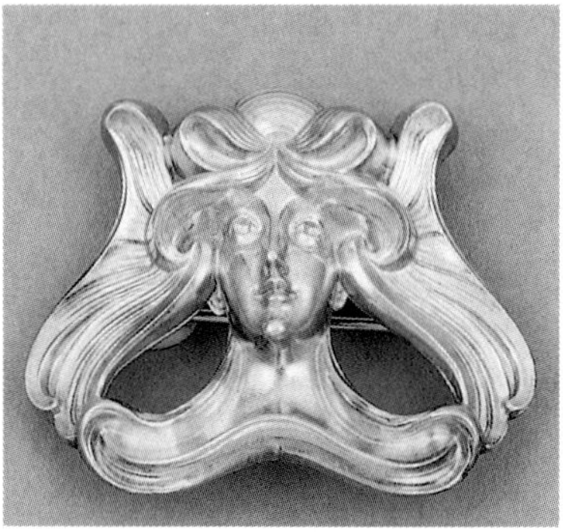

Kerr gilt metal brooch
Width: 6.5cm
Sold: Phillips, London, 21/10/86
Price: £330

JEWELLERY IN AMERICA

The first of the Art Nouveau styles to reach America was the French 'florid' style; this was adapted by mass manufacturers in New Jersey and Providence, both centres for inexpensive jewellery. The firm of Tiffany and Co. was making inventive jewellery in the 1870s but it was not really even early Art Nouveau although there is a Japanese influence in the decorations and motifs of the silver and mixed metal pieces, and in the more expensive jewels made from gold of various colours. It was not until 1900, when Louis Comfort Tiffany, the son of the firm's founder, fascinated by the new style and the ideas developed by the Arts and Crafts guilds in England, turned to making jewellery in the Art Nouveau style. Before that he had been an interior designer and later a glass-maker. The style he evolved combined the abstract shapes of the Liberty designs with organic, natural forms related to those of French design. Like Lalique, he experimented with techniques, including enamelling (his own pieces were costly when they were produced and are now very rare), and he employed designers to work in his studio. These included Julia Munson who evolved her own enamelling techniques for pieces which were produced under the Tiffany name. The influence of the company on Art Nouveau jewellery design in America was significant, although what the company produced itself was generally too expensive to be available to the general public.

Mass manufacturers such as the Gorham Manufacturing Co., which was based in Providence, Rhode Island, produced silver jewellery for the mass market under the name 'Martelé'. The forms and motifs of Martelé are borrowed from the natural shapes of French jewellery but there is a distinctly 'crafted' feel to the pieces which relates to the jewellery of the English Arts and Crafts Movement, which was much admired in America.

Kerr and Co. and the Unger Brothers made inexpensive, mainly silver, jewellery in a style derived almost directly from French design, with the ubiquitous Lalique female profile as a favourite motif. Unger Brothers marketed their designs under the name Philomen Dickinson after 1903. Other firms making jewellery in the Art Nouveau style and marketing it at reasonable prices were Ostby and Barton, of Providence, Blackington and Co. of Massachusetts, and Averbeck and Averbeck, of New York.

BELGIAN AND GERMAN JEWELLERY

Jewellery design in both Belgium and Germany falls into two basic categories. One was influenced by the French 'florid' style, derived from natural forms and often using themes

Unger Brothers brooch
Width: 5.5cm
Sold: Phillips, London, 21/10/86
Price: £275

which relate to Lalique's more bizarre work. At the same time a more abstract and linear style was developed which related more closely to English design than anything being made in France.

In Belgium, Philippe Wolfers, the

Gold, opal, moonstone and *plique-à-jour* enamel necklace
Width: 4cm
Sold: Phillips, London, 21/10/86
Price: £660

Pearl, emerald and enamel pendant
Height: 5.7cm
Sold: Phillips, London, 21/10/86
Price: £330

son of a family of established jewellers, made works in the nineties which were rich, often grotesque and slightly morbid, and incorporated a wide range of precious materials.

The more abstract forms of Art Nouveau were developed in Belgium by the designer Henry van de Velde. The design and manufacture of jewellery was only one of his skills in the applied arts – he was also an architect and furniture designer. Van de Velde's concern was less with the creation of opulent objects than with the expression of linear abstraction. To this end he made jewels which were devoid of surface embellishment, relying instead on designs of powerfully rhythmic forms which were often arranged symmetrically, and on the texturing of the gold and silver with which he worked. His use of stones was deliberately restrained, serving only to accentuate the source of a line or to emphasize the elastic curve of a shape.

In Munich, designers such as Karl Rothmuller, Nikolaus Thallmayr and Erich Erler used the same themes as Wolfers did but interpreted them in a slightly different way. Munich Art Nouveau was generally less bizarre than the French version of the style. One of its major sources of information and inspiration was the magazine *Jugend*, particularly the floral decorations devised for it by the graphic artist August Endell. Endell's work consisted almost entirely of formalized compositions of plant and animal forms but lacked the metamorphosed creatures and fantastic atmosphere of contemporary work in France; the robust quality of his work is echoed in the pieces produced by other Munich-based designers and craftsmen.

Berlin was the centre for a different development; the jewellery trade in that city was deeply conservative and it was left to a few individual designers and manufacturers to develop the new style. The two firms of Louis Werner and J.H. Werner commissioned artists such as Bruno Möhring and Hermann Hirzel to make pieces in a disciplined style, still based on plant forms, but less florid than the jewels made in Munich. Wilhelm Lucas von Cranach designed the most extreme and

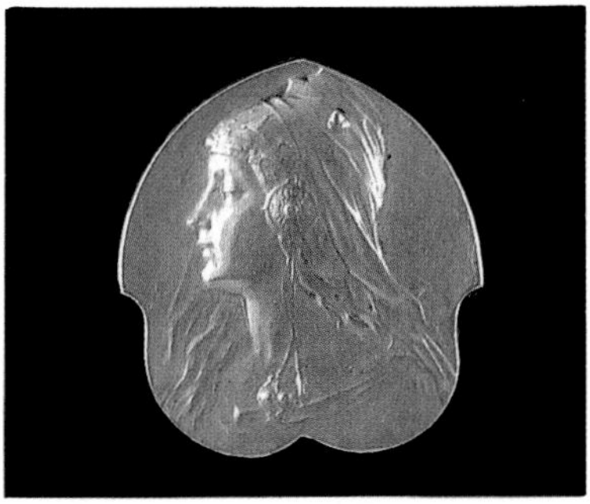

Silver brooch
Width: 3cm
Mark Markov, F1/6 Antiquarius, London
Price: £85

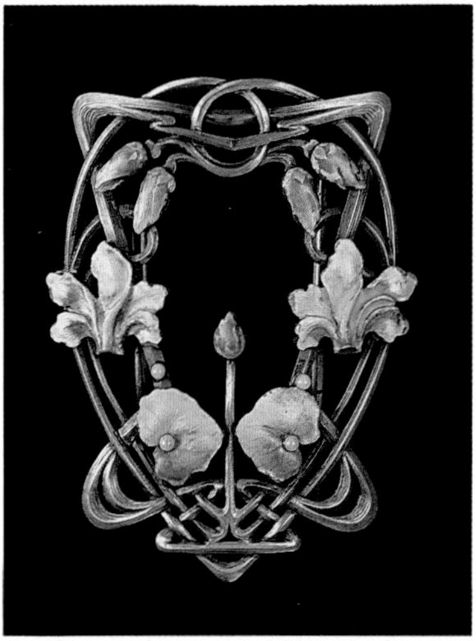

Silver, pearl and enamel buckle
Height: 8.5cm
Keiron and Sabina, N15/16 Antiquarius, London
Price: £450

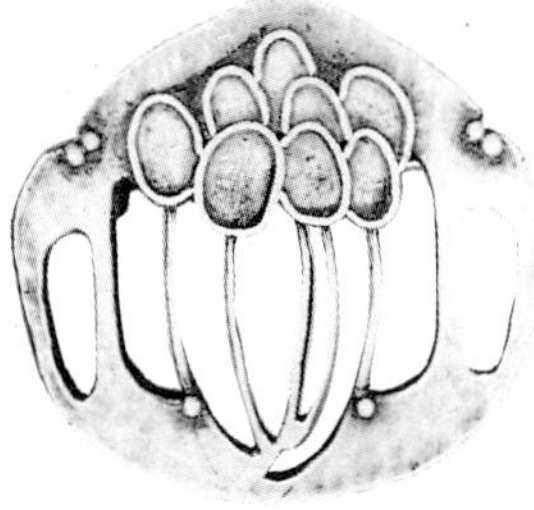

Enamelled brooch
Width: 3cm
Sold: Phillips, London, 21/10/86
Price: £121

exotic pieces to come from Berlin in the nineties. His work was based entirely on plant and animal forms, incorporating the more sinister of these: bats, snakes, owls and winged sea-creatures, made in enamel and carved stone, figure prominently in his designs.

In Germany the centre for the abstract style was the colony at Darmstadt, founded in 1897 by the Grand Duke Ludwig with a view to establishing a permanent home for artists and designers from Germany and elsewhere. The inspiration for Darmstadt came from the English Arts and Crafts movement. and jewellery made at the colony was handcrafted, each piece a unique item. Joseph Maria Olbrich, who was the leading figure in the colony, brought with him ideas which he had developed in Vienna. His style, and that of his friend Peter Behrens, was based on simple elongated shapes made in gold or silver set with strongly coloured blister stones. His unique pieces are rare, but he and other members of the colony also designed for the manufacturer Theodor Fahrner whose workshops were based some 32 km (20 miles) from Darmstadt at Pforzheim, a centre for the mass production of inexpensive jewellery.

Fahrner's impact on Art Nouveau in Germany was considerable. Like Liberty in England he commissioned works from artists and then translated their designs into forms which suited commercial production. Because of his relationship with the colony at Darmstadt most of his output consisted of strong, simple pieces with abstract shapes and almost no reference to the florid style. Ludwig Habich, Olbrich, Patriz Huber, Paul Bürck and Hans Christiansen all designed for Fahrner while they were working at Darmstadt.

Fahrner's stable of designers increased every time he saw an artist whose work he liked. His company also made pieces designed by van de Velde, Moritz Gradl and Georg Kleemann (the latter adapted his early florid style to a more restrained geometric discipline but his work remains the most extravagant produced by Fahrner).

Pforzheim had been a centre for

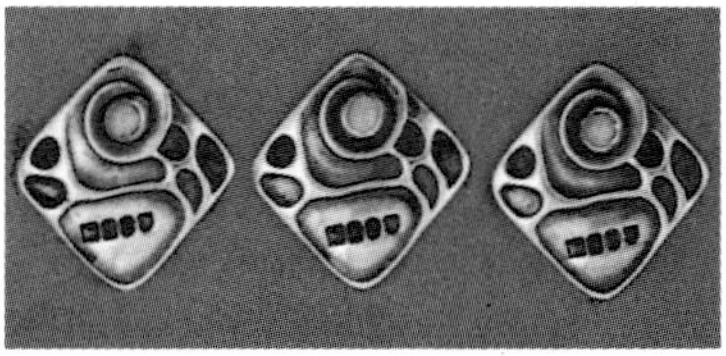

Theodor Fahrner silver and turquoise buttons
1.3 × 1.3cm
Sold: Phillips, London, 21/10/86
Price (6): £198

the production of inexpensive jewellery since the early nineteenth century, but its adoption of Art Nouveau was slow and rather late; the real output of the new style from Pforzheim dates from the end of the nineties. The first Art Nouveau pieces made there were heavily influenced by French design (unsurprisingly, since some French manufacturers actually sent designs to Pforzheim to be made up). The first companies to develop a markedly different and more abstract style were Wilhelm Stoffler, Georg Kolb and F. Zerriner.

AUSTRIAN DESIGN

Austria, or more specifically Vienna, was late in developing new forms in jewellery design. It was not until the formation of the Vienna Secession in 1897 that any design which showed a break with historicism began to emerge. Art Nouveau was already fashionable in the city, and imported jewellery in the style was referred to as the 'genre Lalique', irrespective of the designer who created it. Examples of English and German jewellery in the abstract style were first seen in Vienna as illustrations in the magazine *Ver Sacrum*, and later in the Secessionist exhibition of 1900 when Ashbee's jewellery was shown. By this time some of the young Viennese designers were working in an Art Nouveau style – Moser and Joseph Olbrich were making pieces which were influenced by French work – but after 1900, a new style, based on severe, elongated geometric shapes began to dominate Viennese work.

Josef Hoffmann designed pieces which combined rectangular forms and enamelled chequerboard patterns with stylized flowers; Kolo Moser used entirely abstract shapes, contrasting elongated and sometimes curving lines with clusters of organic ovals, filled with either semi-precious stones or blisters of enamel. Some of his designs were made and marketed by Georg Anton Scheidt in Vienna, while Oskar Dietrich sold the designs. Other designers working in the geometric abstract manner of the Werkstätte were Karl Witzmann, Eduard Wimmer and Bernhard Löffler. Otto Prutscher produced some work in the Werkstätte manner but its severity was softened by the use of coloured enamels and forms derived from nature.

Although Viennese jewellery represents the most extreme point in the development of Art Nouveau in Europe, it was the Viennese linear style that developed most naturally into the geometric shapes of the twenties.

Wiener Werkstätte enamelled metal brooch
Width: 4cm
Sold: Sotheby's, London, 16/5/86
Price: £770

Object	Quality of manufacture	Quality of design and/or decoration	Rarity	Price (£)	Price ($)
Anon.					
diamond and pearl pendant	7	7	■ ■	300–400	480–640
ruby and pearl pendant	7	7	■ ■	150–300	240–480
enamelled brooch	7	7	■ ■	100–200	160–320
diamond and peridot necklace	8	8	■ ■ ■	500–800	800–1280
gold, opal, moonstone and plique-à-jour enamel necklace	8	8	■ ■	600–800	1000–1280
silver gilt, ruby, pearl and plique-à-jour enamel pendant	8	7	■ ■	250–500	400–800
silver, marcasite, pearl and plique-à-jour enamel pendant	8	8	■ ■	450–750	720–1200
silver, pearl and enamel pendant	7	7	■	50–100	80–160
silver and enamel buckle	7	7	■ ■	150–300	240–480
silver, pearl and enamel buckle	8	9	■ ■ ■	300–600	480–1000
silver gilt and plique-à-jour enamel brooch	8	7	■ ■	100–300	160–480
horn brooch	7	7	■	50–100	80–160
horn comb	7	7	■ ■	60–150	96–240
Becker, E.					
gold brooch	8	8	■ ■	500–1000	800–1600
silver brooch	8	8	■ ■	200–600	320–1000
Bonté					
carved horn pendant	7	8	■ ■	100–200	160–320
carved horn brooch	7	8	■ ■	75–150	120–240
Comyns, W.					
silver buckle	7	7	■ ■	100–200	160–320
Dropsy, E.					
silver buckle	7	8	■ ■	100–200	160–320
silver brooch	7	8	■ ■	120–240	192–380

Qualities on a scale 1-10 ■ Rare ■ ■ Very rare ■ ■ ■ Extremely rare

Object	Quality of manufacture	Quality of design and/or decoration	Rarity	Price (£)	Price ($)
Dubois, P.					
silver buckle	8	8	■ ■ ■	500–900	800–1440
Fahrner, T.					
silver and turquoise buttons (6)	8	8	■ ■	150–300	240–480
silver and chalcedony buckle (designed by P. Huber)	8	9	■ ■ ■	400–600	640–1000
silver, opal and enamel brooch (designed by G. Kleemann)	8	8	■ ■ ■	150–300	240–480
Fisher, A.					
silver, opal and enamel buckle	9	9	■ ■ ■	900–1000 +	1440–1600 +
Fouquet, G.					
gold, diamond and pearl pendant (incorporating medallion by S. Vernier)	9	8	■ ■ ■	600–1000	1000–1600
GIP					
carved horn pendant	7	8	■ ■	100–200	160–320
carved horn brooch	7	8	■ ■	75–150	120–240
Gorham					
silver brooch	7	7	■ ■	100–200	160–320
Horner, C.					
silver and mother-of-pearl pendant	7	7	■ ■	75–150	120–240
Kerr, W.					
gilt metal brooch	8	8	■ ■	300–500	480–800
Lalique, R.					
gilt metal and glass brooch	9	9	■ ■ ■	900–1000 +	1440–1600 +

Qualities on a scale 1-10 ■ Rare ■ ■ Very rare ■ ■ ■ Extremely rare

Object	Quality of manufacture	Quality of design and/or decoration	Rarity	Price (£)	Price ($)
Levinger, H.					
silver, amazonite, mother-of-pearl and plique-à-jour enamel brooch	8	7	■■	250–500	400–800
silver, glass and enamel buttons (6)	8	7	■■	200–300	320–480
silver, opal and enamel brooch	8	7	■■	150–250	240–400
Liberty					
'Cymric' silver and enamel buttons (6)	7	8	■	100–200	160–320
turquoise and enamel pendant	7	7	■■	150–300	240–480
gold and mosaic opal ring	8	8	■■■	800–1000	1280–1600
'Cymric' silver and enamel buckle	7	7	■■	150–300	240–480
silver and enamel brooch	7	8	■■	200–400	320–640
Michelsen, C.					
brooch	8	8	■■■	300–600	480–960
pendant	8	8	■■■	400–800	640–1280
comb	8	8	■■■	150–250	240–400
Murat					
brooch	7	7	■■	150–300	240–480
buckle	7	7	■■	150–300	240–480
Murrle Bennett					
gold and pearl pendant	7	7	■■	200–400	320–640
silver and turquoise pendant	7	7	■■	100–200	160–320
Nienhuis, L.					
enamelled brooch	8	8	■■■	350–700	560–1120
Piel Frères					
gilt metal and enamel brooch	7	7	■■	250–500	400–800

Qualities on a scale 1-10 ■ Rare ■■ Very rare ■■■ Extremely rare

Object	Quality of manufacture	Quality of design and/or decoration	Rarity	Price (£)	Price ($)
Plisson & Hartz					
brooch	8	8	■ ■ ■	300–900	480–1440
pendant	8	8	■ ■ ■	400–950	640–1520
Ramsden & Carr					
silver buckle	8	8	■ ■	250–500	400–800
silver and enamel buckle	8	8	■ ■	300–600	480–1000
silver turquoise and enamel pendant	8	8	■ ■ ■	600–1000 +	1000–1600 +
Roty, O.					
silver medal-brooch	8	8	■ ■	300–600	480–960
Scheidt, G.					
brooch	8	8	■ ■	200–500	320–800
Tiffany					
gold, sapphire and moonstone brooch	9	7	■ ■	600–800	1000–1280
Unger Bros					
silver brooch	7	8	■ ■	100–300	160–480
Vernier, S.					
silver medal-pendant	8	8	■ ■	300–600	480–960
Wiener Werkstätte					
enamelled brooch	8	8	■ ■ ■	700–1000 +	1120–1600 +
Zorra, L.					
silver, pearl and enamel pendant	8	8	■ ■ ■	400–800	640–1280

Qualities on a scale 1-10 ■ Rare ■ ■ Very rare ■ ■ ■ Extremely rare

The Yellow Book

An Illustrated Quarterly

Volume II July 1894

London: Elkin Mathews & John Lane
Boston: Copeland & Day

Price 5/- Net

CHAPTER SIX

PRINTS AND POSTERS

The Yellow Book, cover by Aubrey Beardsley. Barbara Stone, J6 Antiquarius, London. Price (complete run of 13 vols): £500.

Although Art Nouveau graphics are associated most strongly with poster design, and although England was somewhat later than the Continent in developing the poster as an art form, it is in England that the first graphic expression of Art Nouveau appeared. It is generally accepted that Arthur Mackmurdo's title page for *Wren's City Churches* published by G. Allen in 1883, with its black and white arabesques and typography mingled with ornament, was the first piece of clearly identifiable Art Nouveau.

Even earlier than Mackmurdo, in the eighteenth century, William Blake combined illustration with text, filling whole pages with rhythmic, curving lines which enclosed and emphasized the lettering, itself much less formal than standard eighteenth-century typography. In 1876 the first retrospective exhibition of Blake's work was held at the Burlington Fine Arts Club in London where it was seen and admired by many of the more forward-looking artists and designers. A monograph on Blake written for the exhibition by Alexander Gilchrist, a friend of Dante Gabriel Rossetti, was popular enough to warrant a second edition in 1880.

Etching by Annie French and G.W. Rhead
22.8 × 20.2cm
Sold: Phillips, London, 19/6/86
Price: £572

Lithographic menu-card by Alphonse Mucha
21 × 14.5cm
Sold: Sotheby's, London, 19/12/86
Price: £143

In the later nineteenth century painters and designers in England and France were influenced by the Japanese woodcut, with its strong emphasis on surface decoration, its lack of formal perspective and its frequent incorporation of text as part of the whole image. In *Hobby Horse*, the magazine first issued by the Century Guild in 1884, Mackmurdo showed his interest in Japanese graphic forms; using the woodcut technique he produced motifs in the form of stylized sunflowers, their petals, stems and leaves reduced to streaming lines of white on black.

BRITISH GRAPHIC STYLE

The work of the innovative graphic artists in England reached its widest public via magazines and periodicals which were also responsible for the dissemination of British ideas on the Continent and in America. In addition to *Hobby Horse*, *The Dial*, founded by Charles Shannon and Charles Ricketts in 1889, regularly displayed new developments in both typography and illustration. Shannon, and more particularly Ricketts, worked in a manner which shows the influence of

Moët & Chandon
Menu
Champagne
Moët & Chandon

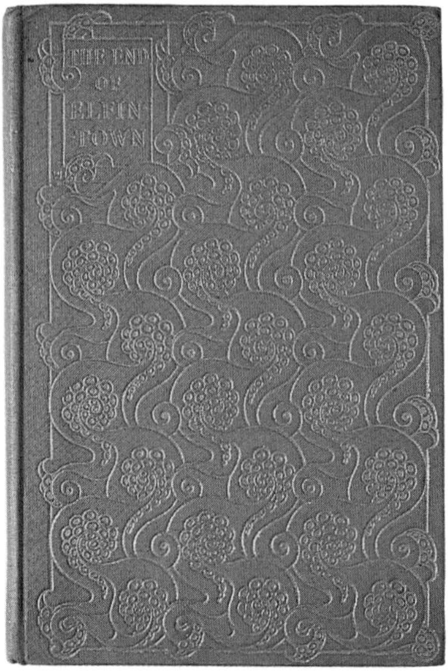

Book cover designed by Laurence Housman
18.2 × 12.5cm
Barbara Stone, J6 Antiquarius, London
Price: £135

the Japanese woodblock print, which almost totally flattens perspective and strengthens tonal contrasts.

The magazine *Studio*, first published in London in 1893, covered all aspects of the decorative arts; in its first year of publication, and in keeping with its policy of featuring the new and innovative designers, it published works by Aubrey Beardsley who was at that time working on his illustrations for *Le Morte d'Arthur* (published by J.M. Dent and Co. in 1893) and as an illustrator for the *Pall Mall Budget*. Beardsley himself was art editor for *The Yellow Book* from 1894 to 1896 and for the magazine *The Savoy* from 1896. Both periodicals are best known for the work which he himself contributed, but both also featured illustrations by lesser-known artists such as William Thomas Horton, Reginald L. Knowles and Fred Hyland, all of whom were working in a style which is recognizably Art Nouveau.

Several private presses were founded in Britain, America and on the Continent in the 1890s. They produced books which were hand set, beautifully produced and often experimental in their use of typography and illustration. The example set by presses such as Ashbee's Essex House Press, Ricketts' Vale Press, and William Morris' Kelmscott Press, certainly influenced the work of the commercial publishers. Bodley Head, Methuen and Co., William Heinemann, George C. Harrap and Co., Clowes and Sons, John Lane and many others were commissioning designs and illustrations for books intended for sale on the popular market. Some of these books were 'Art Nouveau' in that they were illustrated and typeset in a new way with text and pictures combining to make a unified whole; the books produced by Walter Crane for Routledge and Co. are examples of this. But more often a cover and frontispiece would be designed in the new style while the typography and overall layout of the book remained fairly traditional. Beardsley designed covers and frontispieces for several books of this kind, particularly those for John Lane's 'Keynote' series (published in America by Roberts Brothers of Boston) between 1893 and 1896.

With Ricketts, Beardsley was the English illustrator who was most admired on the Continent and in America. His work for books and magazines, and his posters for the theatre and for companies like Singer, show a revolutionary approach to graphic design. His illustrations for *Salome* by Oscar Wilde, published by Lane in 1894, are extraordinary in their lack of perspective and in their arrangement of costume, architectural detail and even the human figure into almost abstract shapes, with areas of dense black and linear decoration set against expanses of white.

The Art Nouveau style was particularly suited to illustrations for fairy tales and fantasy, and indeed it persisted in this area long after the 1914–18 war. The illustrator Walter

Book cover designed by Charles Robinson
19.5 × 13.5cm
Barbara Stone, J6 Antiquarius, London
Price: £28

Book cover designed by Mabel Lucy Attwell
19 × 14.5cm
Trocchi Rare Books Ltd, L8/9 Antiquarius, London
Price: £36

Crane is best remembered in Britain for his work in books such as *The Baby's Opera* (1877), *The Shepheard's Calendar* (1865), *Flora's Feast* (1889) and his *Illustrations for Shakespeare* (1893–94). His graphic work is interesting both formally and in terms of the images he developed before the 1890s. Like Beardsley he made little use of perspective, often dividing a panel horizontally into bands of different tones which he linked with a curving vertical, a plant or a human figure. The borders of his pictures were seldom simple lines; they developed instead into organic plant shapes which then

became part of the image. In addition, he frequently incorporated text into his illustrations. The archetypal Art Nouveau image of the human figure mutating into plant or insect form appeared in many of his illustrations from the 1880s and 1890s. Crane's influence was considerable both in America, where he lectured in 1891, and in Europe, which he toured extensively.

Arthur Rackham used the pictorial and formal language of Art Nouveau in a rather different way in his illustrations for fairy and fantasy stories. Apart from his complex and detailed pictures for books like Washington Irving's *Rip Van Winkle* or Grimm's *Fairy Tales* he developed a technique for making images in silhouette. Ultimately these derive from Japanese cut-out paper pictures, but Rackham used black ink, occasionally contrasting it with shapes in pink or sage green, and transforming trees, human figures, buildings and fantas-

Lithographic calendar by Alphonse Mucha
31.4 × 14cm (each)
Sold: Sotheby's, New York, 6/12/86
Price: $1210

tic creatures into strongly decorative and rhythmic flat shapes. Rackham's silhouettes have more to do with Art Nouveau graphics than his colour work did, which, despite its considerable charm, was fairly orthodox in its deployment of figures in space and use of perspective.

The best poster designs in England were produced by the Beggarstaff Brothers – William Nicholson and James Pryde. Nicholson was largely self-taught although he attended the Académie Julian in Paris for a short time. From the mid-nineties he and Pryde produced a series of posters for the theatre (including the famous *Don Quixote* for the Lyceum), and for commercial products and magazines. Using woodcuts, the Beggarstaffs made images which combined simplified and dramatic shapes with strong tonal and colour contrasts. Under his own name Nicholson produced portfolios of smaller prints, including *Twelve Portraits* (of Queen Victoria, Sarah Bernhardt and Bismark, among others) and *London Types*. Like Lautrec, in France, Nicholson had an eye for the minimum amount of detail necessary to convey information about a character. His Sarah Bernhardt, for instance, is instantly recognizable; he has isolated her piled mass of hair and white face against a framing black cape, eliminating all other details, so that the silhouette of her costume reads as a dramatic shape against the neutral tones of the curtain behind her. Nicholson's work and that of the Beggarstaffs is still reasonably priced, with the exception of some of their most famous designs, such as *Don Quixote* and the posters for the magazine *Harper's*.

Dudley Hardy, who also worked on posters for the London theatres in the 1890s, produced designs which show a French influence in their expression of movement; his *Gaiety Girl* poster for the Prince of Wales Theatre (1894) with its formalized, and swirling lines owes a particular debt to the graphic style of the most prominent French poster designer, Jules Chéret.

DESIGN IN AMERICA

It is impossible to overestimate the role of magazines and periodicals in the exchange of ideas and spread of information which is so characteristic of the 1890s. In America, for example, William Bradley was recog-

nized as one of the best draughtsmen and illustrators of the nineties, working for the *Chicago Tribune*, *Echo* and *The Inland Printer* as an illustrator and a poster designer. *Studio* published an article on Bradley illustrated with examples of his poster designs in 1895, as a direct result of which he was invited to exhibit at the first exhibition at Siegfried Bing's shop and gallery in Paris, La Maison de l'Art Nouveau. Bradley himself founded his own Wayside Press in Springfield in 1895 and published several magazines including *Bradley:*

His Book which contained his own work and that of other illustrators working in the new manner.

Will Bradley was preceded, but not particularly influenced, by the painter Elihu Vedder who designed Christmas cards and in 1884 illustrated the *Rubaiyat of Omar Khayyam*. Vedder's graphic style, like that of some of his English contemporaries such as Selwyn Image and Mackmurdo, owed a considerable amount to illustrations by William Blake.

The china-painter Louis John Rhead, uncle of Frederick Hurten Rhead and Charlotte Rhead, emigrated from Britain to the USA in 1883. He designed bookbindings for the New York bookbinder William Matthews, and in 1894 started making original posters in the Art

***Dreaming*, photogravure by Maxfield Parrish**
16.2 × 25.6cm
David Rayner, N4/5 Antiquarius, London
Price: £35

***Sarah Bernhardt*, lithograph**
by Paul Berthon
55.5 × 40.5cm
Sold: Sotheby's, London, 19/12/86
Price: £264

Nouveau style. His work was widely acclaimed and in 1897 the Salon des Cent in Paris held an exhibition of his lithographic posters.

Edward Penfield, whose work was generously commended by Will Bradley, designed posters for the magazine *Harper's* in a style related to that of the Swiss artist Théophile-Alexandre Steinlen. Other successful American poster arists were Will Carqueville, who worked for the magazine *Lippincott's*, and Ethel Reed. Both Maxfield Parrish and Joseph C. Leyendecker began their careers working in an Art Nouveau manner, although their work is more usually associated with later styles.

THE GLASGOW SCHOOL

The fantastic alliance of human and abstract form played an important part in the work of Margaret Macdonald, who trained at the Glasgow School of Art and worked first as a designer for metalwork and embroidery. Her graphic work incorporated the stylized human forms she had used in her designs for applied art; they were elongated, geometric and abstract shapes, usually in black and white with one or two isolated colour areas – a rose perhaps, or a series of coloured rectangles. From 1900, when she married the architect and designer Charles Rennie Mackintosh, her work was done mainly in collaboration with him and there are obvious influences from each on the others' graphic work. For example, Mackintosh's poster designs for *The Scottish Musical Review* (1896) demonstrate the same elongated forms, flat colour and formalized human shapes that his wife used. Both Mackintosh and Macdonald had a considerable influence on the development of Art Nouveau in Austria where this geometric aspect of the style flourished in the work of the Wiener Werkstätte.

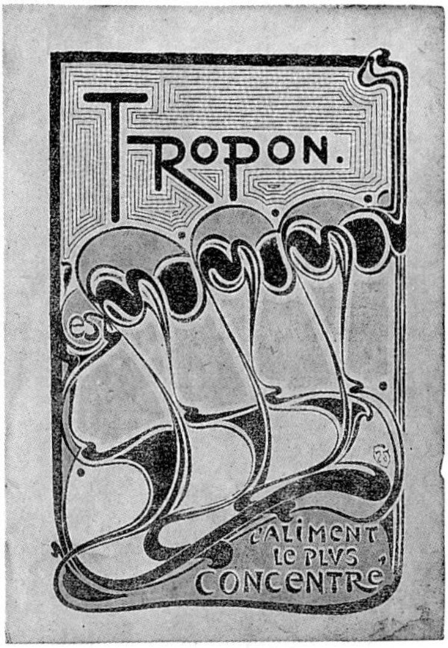

Lithograph by Henry van de Velde from *L'Art décoratif*
27.5 × 12cm
Sold: Sotheby's, London, 19/12/86
Price: £198

Jessie M. King, who also trained at Glasgow, devised illustrations for books produced by the private presses and by commercial publishers (such as the *Defence of Guinevere*, issued by John Lane, 1904), as well as designing a number of small-scale graphic works such as Ex Libris plates. Essentially her work was not suitable for poster design, since she relied on fine lines and stippled detail and seldom used the contrasts of tone or colour or the clear shapes that make it possible to understand a poster at a distance.

GRAPHIC ART IN FRANCE

Despite the proliferation of information about graphic style in the 1890s and the mobility of the artists themselves, there is not (as one might expect) a conformity of style. There are elements which link the art of England with that of France, and Austrian graphics with the art of Belgium or Germany, and it is certainly true that there is an international movement in design that we can identify as 'Art Nouveau', but it developed differently in each country where influences and ideas fed into the existing traditions in the arts.

In France the mysterious and romantic images of the Pre-Raphaelites and the graphic developments of the Arts and Crafts movement, together with the pervasive influence of Japanese art, were mixed with ideas and forms that originated in the work of the Pont-Aven painters Paul Gauguin and Emile Bernard. In the late 1880s Gauguin and Bernard had developed a method of picture construction using simplified shapes and flat, non-representational colours, and both painters had dispensed with formal perspective.

The Pont-Aven painters had a major influence on the young artists Maurice Denis, Paul Sérusier, Paul Ranson, Pierre Bonnard and Edouard Vuillard, who formed the core of the Paris-based group called the Nabis (prophets). The expressive use of line and colour and rejection of perspective in the work of the Nabis gave it a visual power, which was recognized by Thadée Natanson, the publisher of the literary magazine *La Revue Blanche*. Originally, the magazine was intended as an outlet for poets, for works of literary criticism, reviews of new books and musical compositions and so on, but Natanson commissioned the Nabis to produce illustrations specifically for the magazine and, in addition, published portfolios of their work as a supplement to the *Revue*. By the middle of the 1890s all the Nabis were producing graphic works. These took the form of either limited editions which were exhibited and sold at Ambroise Vollard's gallery (as was Maurice Denis' series *Amour* in 1898), one of the major outlets for Art Nouveau graphics, or illustrations for books or magazines, or posters for the new theatres in Paris, particularly the Théâtre de l'Œuvre, the Théâtre des Pantins, the Théâtre de l'Art and the Théâtre Libre.

Pierre Bonnard was perhaps the best poster designer of all the Nabis. He used a method of picture construction derived from the Japanese print and the Pont-Aven painters with backgrounds described as horizontal or diagonal bands, with the figures (often in silhouette) placed at the extreme edges of the composition. In his posters for *La Revue Blanche* and Le Salon des Cent he incorporated typography as part of the image, producing a poster which conveyed its information quickly while still retaining its impact as an image.

By the time that the influence of ideas from the fine arts, from Japanese prints and from English graphics began to make their impact on French graphic design, Jules Chéret had already been established as the leading poster designer in Europe for twenty years. He had owned his own lithographic workshop in Paris since 1866 and had evolved a style which remained consistent, except for a short period in the early nineties. Chéret's training had been entirely within the lithographic workshops in

The Lute-players, photogravure by Maxfield Parrish
15.5 × 25.5cm
David Rayner, N4/5 Antiquarius, London
Price: £35

Paris and London where he learned his trade; he attended no formal art schools or academies but still produced posters which, at their best, were the most powerful evocations of the *belle époque.* His images for Saxoleine Petrole (1891–92), Job cigarette papers (1895), Dubonnet (1895), the Folies-Bergère, and his numerous dust-jackets, were composed of atmospheric colours from which fragments of background and isolated 'telling' objects emerge, against which his figures dance.

Chéret's output was prodigious; he produced more than 1,000 designs in his working life and his influence was considerable. Because his style was so evocative it was imitated by designers in many countries with varying success. The methods of composition which Chéret used, particularly his dynamic use of typography, became hackneyed in the hands of less skilful draughtsmen. Chéret's work is mostly innaccessible to the ordinary collector. Despite his output, little of his original work survives; it was, after all, designed to be displayed on billboards, to be torn down and replaced after a few weeks.

Théophile-Alexandre Steinlen was also established as a graphic artist in Paris from the beginning of the 1880s; he worked mainly for newspapers and journals including *La Caricature, Le Chat Noir* (a newspaper issued by the management of the Montmartre café of the same name) and *Gil Blas Illustré*; his work did not become explicitly Art Nouveau until the 1890s when he responded to the formal ideas in Lautrec's poster designs. But he adapted them to his more sinuous and elegant line.

Henri de Toulouse-Lautrec knew

and admired the Nabis and exhibited with them at Le Barc de Boutteville in Paris in 1892; he also collaborated with Henri-Gabriel Ibels (who joined the Nabis in 1889) on a portfolio of prints called *Le Café Concert*, published in 1893. Some of his techniques of picture construction and his use of lithographic texture can be related to Bonnard's, but Lautrec,

Lithographic poster by Privat Livemont
69 × 36cm
Sold: Sotheby's, London, 19/12/86
Price: £880

***L'Heure du berger*, chromolithograph by Hans Christiansen**
35.5 × 22.3cm
Sold: Phillips, London, 13/3/86
Price: £220

like Beardsley, made everything he learned and used uniquely his own. While he was certainly not the first poster designer in Paris, the thirty-two posters he produced, for cabaret artists such as Aristide Bruant and Yvette Guilbert, for café-cabarets such as the Moulin Rouge, and for periodicals including *La Revue Blanche*, demonstrate his absolute understanding of the basic function of the poster. His images are strong and essentially two-dimensional and can be read from a distance without losing their meaning. Most importantly he could create exactly the atmosphere required by his various clients; his posters for Bruant, with their dramatic silhouette and only the face shown in any detail, evoke the powerful and dominating persona that was the performer's particular appeal. Lautrec created a different visual shorthand for Yvette Guilbert using stark black, white and orange, and line rather than silhouette, to evoke an atmosphere of jaded artificiality. He was able to command high prices for his work even as a relative newcomer to poster design simply because his images worked.

The imagery of Art Nouveau is inseparable from that of Symbolism; the dreaming women and fantastic plants and landscapes evoked in the work of poets such as Mallarmé also appear in graphic works made specifically to advertise commercial products or events. The women in the

posters designed by Alphonse Mucha (born in Moravia but working in Paris in the 1890s), Manuel Orazi and Georges de Feure are not simply pretty women: Mucha's robust nymphs, with impossibly abundant hair which coils out in serpentine lines to fill the picture surface, were often engaged in modern activities (rolling cigarettes, for example, in his posters for Job cigarette papers), but they are still related to Rossetti's Proserpines – exotic, dangerous and not entirely of this world. De Feure and Orazi both used images of women in contemporary costume and in a similar way, with the hands and faces as pale shapes against exaggerated hairstyles, feathered hats and immense sweeping skirts. These women do not specifically advertise a product or place, they are intended to convey a mood of refined and slightly decadent elegance. De Feure studied under Chéret in the 1890s adapting Chéret's lithographic techniques to his own style and making posters for the Salon des Cent, Loïe Fuller and the Thermes Liègeois.

Eugène Grasset and his pupil Paul Berthon both designed posters which incorporated Symbolist imagery and a style which derives in part from Burne-Jones and Walter Crane, with innovative typography. Grasset designed his own type for his book *Histoire des Quatre Fils Aymon* published in 1883, and his 'Grasset' alphabet, first produced in 1898, became used by several commercial printers in France. His posters, and Berthon's, are more formal in their structure than either Chéret's or Lautrec's and more directly narrative in their images. Berthon's work is usually within the average collector's reach, but prices for Grasset's are often very high.

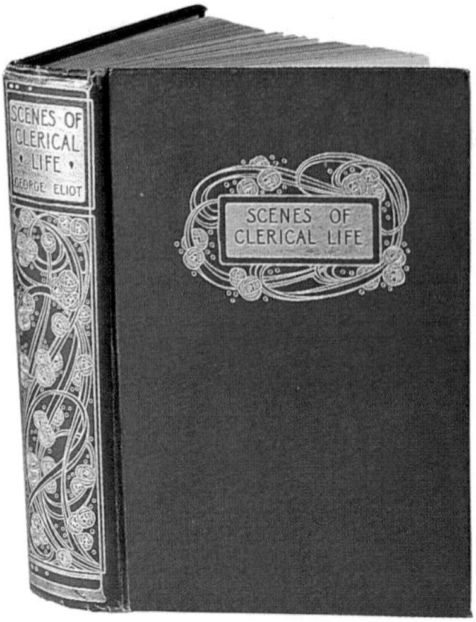

Book cover in the Glasgow style
20.2 × 14.5cm
Trocchi Rare Books Ltd,
L8/9 Antiquarius, London
Price: £13

BELGIAN GRAPHICS

In Belgium the Cercle des Vingt (Circle of Twenty) was a Brussels-based group of artists who produced illustrations and posters. Symbolism was an important element in their work, particularly for Fernand Khnopff who was influenced by the work of Burne-Jones and the French painter Gustave Moreau. In the illustrations which Khnopff contributed to the German magazine *Pan* and the Viennese *Ver Sacrum*, he used an image of a sphinx-like woman, which also appears in his paintings; in his graphic work she is formalized to become almost mask-like and often set against a linear background.

Henry van de Velde, the Belgian painter, architect and furniture designer who was a founder member of the Cercle des Vingt, produced some graphic work in the 1890s including a poster for the Tropon company in 1898. Unlike the contemporary posters in France the Tropon poster used no image but instead relied on an arrangement of completely abstract linear shapes which rise from the base of the design to meet a rectilinear maze which contains the word 'Tropon' in a formalized typeface. Van de Velde abandoned the use of pictorial images in his graphic works, and his decorative borders are based on pure, decorative line derived from his own theories of dynamic and harmonious curves. His typography was related to the same theory and thus had a natural connection with the decoration – the 'Tropon' poster is a demonstration of the success of his theory.

The work of Privat Livemont, who studied in Paris before returning to work in Belgium in 1889, offers a complete contrast to that of van de Velde since it relies on the evocative power of the image. His style was very similar to Mucha's and his range of imagery included the same voluptuous nudes or semi-nudes with backgrounds created from stylized plant forms or the hair of the central image. It was a style which was popular with manufacturers, and Privat Livemont made posters for 'Cacao Van Houten', 'Café Rajah' and many other products in the nineties.

Other Belgian designers – Henri Meunier, Adolphe Crespin and Fernand Toussaint, all of whom made posters in a style with a strong French influence – were successful commercially and had their designs collected by Belgian connoisseurs who bought them as they would buy paintings or limited edition prints.

DUTCH GRAPHIC ART

The Dutch Symbolist painters Jan Toorop and Jan Thorn-Prikker were both associated with the Cercle des

Lithographic trade card by Privat Livemont
12 × 26cm
Pruskin Gallery, London
Price: £50

Vingt and both worked in highly personal styles which bear little resemblance to anything produced in France or Belgium in the 1890s. Toorop's posters for 'Delftsche Slaolie', designed in 1895, incorporated the human figure but were still uncompromisingly two-dimensional; the drapery, hair and plant forms are all pulled into complex linear patterns so that the whole surface of the poster becomes animated. Toorop was born and spent his childhood in Java where his father was an official of the Dutch government, and his style of two-dimensional formalization has something in common with Indonesian textile designs.

Thorn-Prikker also worked in a linear style which, like Toorop's, is two-dimensional but less decorative in its overall effect. His posters for 'Revue Bimestrielle pour l'Art Appliqué', (1896) and the Dutch Art Exhibition of 1903 are Art Nouveau certainly, but with a tendency towards Expressionism which became more marked in his later work, particularly when he was teaching in Munich and Dusseldorf.

GRAPHIC ART IN GERMANY

Art Nouveau, or Jugendstil as it was called in Germany, developed mainly in two centres – Berlin and Munich. Almost all the artists working in Germany in the 1890s seem to have visited these two cities at some point in their careers and there was a free interchange of ideas across the country. Nevertheless it is possible to see influences becoming personalized in the hands of individual artists. Beardsley's influence is evident in the works of Markus Behmer and Thomas Theodor Heine who founded *Simplicissimus*, a satirical magazine, in Munich; it can be seen too in illustrations by Olaf Gulbransson who also worked for *Simplicissimus*. Baron Vogt, who worked under the pseudonym 'Alastair,' took Beardsley's eroticism to an extreme. The simplified shapes and stressed outlines of the Nabis were adapted by Hans Christiansen, Ludwig von Zumbusch and Josef Sattler, while Ludwig Hohlwein and Hans Rudi Erdt adapted the techniques of the Beggarstaffs for their own posters.

Many young artists from Berlin and Munich spent some time in Paris, and *La Revue Blanche* was distributed in Germany; at the same time *Studio* was bringing British design to the attention of German artists, and van de Velde was developing ideas which had considerable impact on German graphic art.

The Berlin Free Association of Artists was founded in 1893 in opposition to the somewhat rigid dictates of the Academy and the magazine with which it was associated was *Pan*. Peter Behrens, Otto Eckmann, Ludwig von Hofmann, Walter Leistikow, August Endell and Josef Satt-

3 prints by C.O. Czeschka
13.5 × 12cm (each)
Sold: Sotheby's, New York, 11/10/86
Price: $357

Lithographic poster by Hans Rudi Erdt
62.5 × 85.5cm
Sold: Sotheby's, New York, 20/6/86
Price: $1320

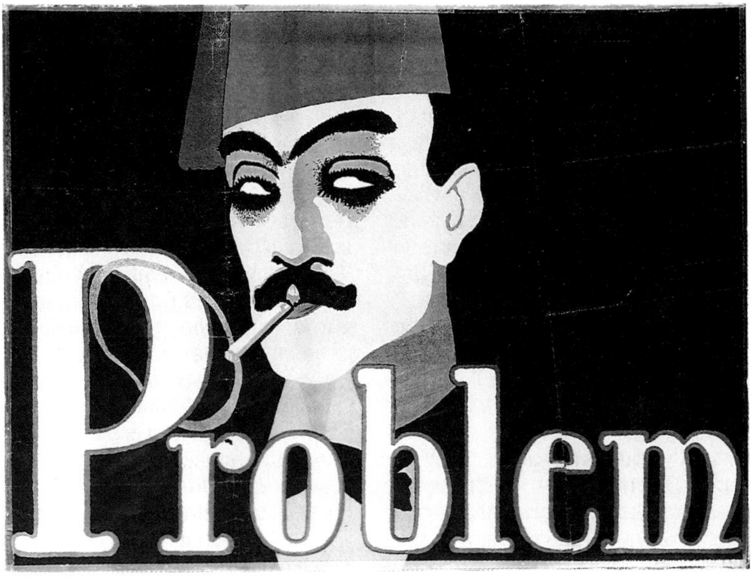

ler were all employed as illustrators for the magazine and all worked in a way which is clearly Art Nouveau, using linear patterns derived from plant forms. The tone of *Pan* was somewhat didactic, and it is interesting that artists such as Eckmann, who also worked for the Munich magazine *Jugend*, employed a different and more experimental style for the latter

Pan aimed for a unified and coherent image and Behrens and Eckmann helped to achieve this. They both developed new typographic forms in the 1890s which were based on organic rather than geometric shapes and both were concerned that text and image should be in harmony in both books and posters. In contrast, *Jugend* was less disciplined in its overall appearance, which changed with almost every issue: Diez's cover in 1899 was derived from Greek vase painting and embossed in gold on grey linen; Franz von Stuck's cover was almost expressionist with dancing figures, and the title 'Jugend' was made to look like mosaic; Ludwig von Zumbusch's offering of the same year, which also shows dancing figures, was drawn in flat colours with strong outlines and with typography that was so organic as to be almost illegible. Several sorts of typography were used in each issue and the contributing artists tended to be experimental in their work. Artists from abroad were invited to contribute to *Jugend*: the Frenchman Jossot was a frequent contributor, as were Shannon and Sturge Moore from England.

AUSTRIAN GRAPHICS

In Austria, avant-garde artists tended to gravitate to Vienna, where the Secession was founded in 1897 to set up a body of artists in opposition to the established Künstlerhaus. The publication *Ver Sacrum* was, like *La Revue Blanche*, a journal which welcomed contributions from both writers and artists. Visually *Ver Sacrum* was very different; its emphasis was on clarity of form, and this in fact characterized Viennese Art Nouveau, which was dominated by a crisp, linear quality and a tendency towards more geometrical shapes as opposed to the florid, organic forms of most French and Belgian work. The influence of the Glasgow School was particularly strong in Vienna and can be seen clearly in the work of Josef Hoffmann. The illustrations Hoffmann produced for *Ver Sacrum* show elongated linear forms contrasted with small areas of black; his typography was based on the same forms, which can also be seen in the work of Margaret Macdonald and Charles Rennie Mackintosh. Kolo Moser used Mackintosh's combination of geometric abstraction and human form in his designs for *Ver Sacrum* and in his posters for the Secession's exhibitions.

It is interesting that the clarity of Viennese Art Nouveau remains apparent even when colour is used; Josef Auchentaller habitually isolated his colour areas against white and stressed the outlines of his plant or human forms so that the colour is contained and controlled; if he used

Decorative design, lithograph by Max Benirschke
29.3 × 25.2cm
Pruskin Gallery, London
Price: £120

typography with text, as he did in his *Ver Sacrum* work, the text is contained within a frame which separates it from the border, the relationship between text and decoration being established by the black outlines. Friedrich König and Leopold Stolba used simple, flat areas of colour which act as a foil for the linear forms which pass across them. Both were members of the Secession group and regular contributors to *Ver Sacrum*.

Ultimately it was the control and architectural quality of Viennese Art Nouveau which ensured its survival; the more flamboyant forms of French Art Nouveau were becoming hackneyed in the first years of the twentieth century, but the clarity of Hoffmann's work provided one of the lasting foundations for modern design.

Object	Quality of manufacture	Quality of design and/or decoration	Rarity	Price (£)	Price ($)
Andri, F.					
lithographic poster	7	8	■■■	800–1000 +	1280–1600 +
woodcut	8	8	■■■	200–400	320–640
Anon.					
lithographic poster	6	7	■	200–600	320–1000
book/magazine illustration	6	7	■	40–80	60–130
Auchentaller, J.					
magazine illustration	7	8	■■■	100–300	160–480
Bastard, M.					
lithographic poster	6	8	■	150–500	240–800
Beardsley, A.					
The Yellow Book (13 vols)	6	10	■■	400–600	640–1000
Salome (not 1st edition)	6	10	■■	150–250	240–400
book/magazine illustration	6	10	■■	50–100	80–160
lithographic poster	6	10	■■■	500–1000 +	800–1600 +
Beggarstaff Brothers					
lithographic poster	6	9	■■■	800–1000 +	1280–1600 +
album	6	9	■■	200–600	320–1000
book illustration	6	9	■	25–50	45–80
Behmer, M.					
woodcut	8	8	■■■	300–900	480–1440
Berthon, P.					
lithograph	6	8	■	250–500	400–800
lithographic poster	6	8	■■	300–600	480–1000

Qualities on a scale 1-10 ■ Rare ■■ Very rare ■■■ Extremely rare

Object	Quality of manufacture	Quality of design and/or decoration	Rarity	Price (£)	Price ($)
Bistolfi, L.					
lithographic poster	6	8	■ ■ ■	500–1000 +	800–1600 +
Bradley, W.					
lithographic poster	6	9	■ ■ ■	600–1000 +	1000–1600 +
book/magazine illustration	6	9	■ ■	200–600	320–1000
Bürck, P.					
woodcut	8	8	■ ■ ■	200–600	320–960
Cappiello, L.					
lithographic poster	6	9	■ ■	400–1000 +	640–1600 +
Chéret, J.					
lithographic poster	7	9	■ ■	800–1000 +	1280–1600 +
Christiansen, H.					
lithograph	7	8	■ ■	200–400	320–640
woodcut	8	8	■ ■	350–750	560–1200
Czeschka, C.					
print	7	8	■ ■	100–300	160–480
Denis, M.					
lithographic poster	6	8	■ ■	200–800	320–1280
Deutsch, E.					
lithographic poster	6	8	■ ■	600–1000 +	1000–1600 +
Endell, F.					
colour woodcut	8	8	■ ■ ■	250–500	400–800

Qualities on a scale 1-10 ■ Rare ■ ■ Very rare ■ ■ ■ Extremely rare

Object	Quality of manufacture	Quality of design and/or decoration	Rarity	Price (£)	Price ($)
Erdt, H.					
lithographic poster	6	7	■■	600–1000 +	1000–1600 +
Fidus					
lithograph	7	8	■■■	200–400	320–640
French, A.					
etching	8	7	■■	300–750	480–1200
Grasset, E.					
pochoir print	8	9	■■	150–300	240–480
lithographic poster	6	9	■■■	800–1000 +	1280–1600 +
Hardy, D.					
lithographic poster	6	8	■■■	600–1000 +	1000–1600 +
Hofmann, L. von					
lithographic magazine illustration	7	8	■■■	100–250	160–400
Hohlwein, L.					
lithograph	6	8	■■	400–800	640–1280
lithographic poster	6	8	■■	800–1000 +	1280–1600 +
Housman, L.					
book cover	9	9	■■■	100–200	160–320
King, J.					
etching	8	8	■■	500–1000	800–1600
Leistikow, W.					
lithographic magazine illustration	7	8	■■■	100–250	160–400

Qualities on a scale 1-10 ■ Rare ■■ Very rare ■■■ Extremely rare

Object	Quality of manufacture	Quality of design and/or decoration	Rarity	Price (£)	Price ($)
Mucha, A.					
lithographic menu card	6	9	■■	100–250	160–400
lithographic calendar	6	9	■■■	750–1000	1200–1600
Orazi, M.					
lithographic poster	6	9	■■	500–1000 +	800–1600 +
Parrish, M.					
photogravure	7	8	■	30–100	48–160
Penfield, E.					
lithographic poster	6	8	■■	250–750	400–1200
Privat Livemont					
lithographic poster	6	9	■■■	750–1000 +	1200–1600 +
lithographic trade card	6	9	■■	50–150	80–240
Reed, E.					
lithographic poster	6	8	■■	200–600	320–1000
Sattler, J.					
book illustration	7	8	■■■	100–300	160–480
Stolba, L.					
woodcut	8	8	■■■	200–400	320–640
van de Velde, H.					
lithographic magazine illustration	7	9	■■■	150–300	240–480
Vogeler, H.					
book illustration	7	8	■■■	100–300	160–480

Qualities on a scale 1-10 ■ Rare ■■ Very rare ■■■ Extremely rare

CHAPTER SEVEN

FURNITURE AND TEXTILES

Mirror by Carlo Bugatti. Sold: Sotheby's, London, 16/5/86. Price: £990.

Dining table, oak
Length: 112.3cm
Furniture Store, London
Price: £280

In 1851 the Great Exhibition was held in London to show the best examples of design and manufacture from all countries. Its extensive catalogue reveals some astonishing developments in manufacturing techniques and an almost universal preoccupation with revivalist design in all areas of the applied arts. Furniture and textiles exhibited a range of historical styles from Gothic and Jacobean to baroque, and styles which were an amalgam of all these. Textiles and carpets were characterized by an aggressively three-dimensional use of pattern in the strong, bright colours of chemical pigments. Contemporary literature expressed enthusiasm for the Exhibition as a whole and there were very few dissenting voices which criticized the lack of originality in design or the inappropriate adaptations of historical styles to modern production methods.

THE ENGLISH STYLE

William Morris, who was one of the dissenters, believed that there should be a return to craftsman production and to simple, functional, vernacular design. From 1859, his firm of Morris, Marshall, Faulkner and Co. was producing sturdy, solidly made furniture to the designs of Philip Webb, but these pieces are less important to the development of Art Nouveau than Morris and Webb's concept of unified design – the idea that furniture, textiles, wallpapers and architecture should have a 'look' in common and that interiors should be designed as a harmonious whole rather than a jumble of mixed styles. Their ideas were disseminated via magazines such as *Studio* and had an important influence in America and on the Continent.

Arthur Heygate Mackmurdo, in his work for the Century Guild, used an emphatically linear style in all his designs; his furniture, textiles and graphic works share the same rhythmic complexity as early as the beginning of the 1880s and his work can be seen as early Art Nouveau. Mackmurdo's work incorporated and translated an important influence on Art Nouveau, that of Japanese art, which first reached Britain in 1862 at the International Exhibition. The simplicity and asymmetry of Japanese design was in marked contrast to anything produced in Europe at this time and the 1862 Exhibition marks the beginning of what was to become an assimilation of Japanese forms and motifs into Western applied arts.

Liberty & Co. opened in 1875 selling Japanese and Oriental goods to supply a growing demand among the fashionable public; in the nineties it began to extend its range to include items designed in a modern style. The firm's first successes were with textiles. John Llewellyn was director of the textile department before being appointed to the board of Liberty in 1898, and he commissioned designs from a range of artists, many of whom had trained or were working with the Arts and Crafts guilds.

Chair, oak, by William Birch
Height: 101cm
Furniture Store, London
Price (set of 4): £875

Arthur Silver (who designed the 'Peacock Feather' fabric), Charles Francis Annesley Voysey, Jessie M. King, Harry Napper, J. Scarratt-Rigby and Lindsay P. Butterfield all worked for Llewellyn designing textiles which, although varied and individual, all show evidence of the Liberty style. On the whole Liberty textiles were characterized by a strongly rhythmic use of pattern, an emphasis on two-dimensional treatment of the surface and a marked use of outline. G.P. and J. Baker and the Rossendale Printing Co. were responsible for the manufacture of many of Liberty's textile designs, using machine roller printing for both furnishing and dress fabrics. Liberty still markets a selection of its original designs and on the occasion of its centenary re-issued Arthur Silver's 'Peacock Feather'.

The Furnishing and Decorative Studio at Liberty was established in 1883 under the direction of Leonard Wyburd. The first pieces of furniture sold in the Studio were made in the workshops of Ursin Fortier in Soho and show a marked Oriental influence. Later, Wyburd imported some pieces from the Continent and their designs were adapted by Liberty's own (and mainly anonymous) artists. Wyburd himself was responsible for some of the company's most popular items of furniture; the three-legged 'Wylye' tea table, its top decorated with a marquetry pattern of stylized poppies, is generally accepted as being one of his designs and is based on the 'Thebes' stool sold by Liberty from 1884. The architect M.H. Baillie-Scott, who designed the dining and drawing rooms for the Grand Duke's Palace at Darmstadt, worked for John White of Bedford who sold to Liberty & Co.

Although Liberty himself rejected the Continental forms of Art Nouveau and was scathing about what he described as 'the fantastic motif which it pleases our Continental friends to worship as l'art nouveau', Liberty furniture from the turn of the century shows every evidence of a restrained form of the style. Although the pieces remained, on the whole, symmetrical and geometric in outline, they do show the elongation of form characteristic of British Art Nouveau and the use of organic, plant-derived motifs as inlay and as hinges, handles and leading on glass doors. Mother-of-pearl and abalone shell were favourite inlays often used in conjunction with marquetry work in coloured woods.

The same simple lines and use of inlay characterized the furniture produced by the firm of J.S. Henry & Co. for which both W.A.S. Benson and Frank Brangwyn designed. The collaboration between designer and industry was particularly important in the dissemination of the new style in Britain; both Benson and Brangwyn worked for Morris and Co. designing craftsman-built and unique pieces of furniture and metalwork, but both were able to adapt their ideas to the demands of mass production. Similarly, C.F.A. Voysey designed carpets, fabrics and hangings for mass production for Alexander Morton (later Morton Sundour) and fabrics for Wylie and Lochhead.

Display cabinet, mahogany with marquetry
Height: 180.5cm
Sold: Christie's South Kensington, London, 19/9/86
Price: £715

THE GLASGOW SCHOOL

The Glasgow School of Art produced a generation of designers who worked in a style that was quite distinct from anything produced elsewhere in Britain. The Glasgow Four – Charles Rennie Mackintosh, Herbert MacNair and Margaret and Frances Macdonald – designed in a way which avoided any period references and which employed only a very restrained surface decoration. Mackintosh's furniture was characterized by its elongated forms and tense, tapering lines and much of his best work was produced as part of his architectural and decorative schemes in and around Glasgow at the turn of the century. The influence of the Glasgow Four was more important on the Continent, particularly in Vienna, than in England where their work, especially their furniture and graphic designs, was felt to be too *outré* and too demanding. Mackintosh's furniture worked visually only in uncluttered, plain interiors of the sort he designed and did not lend itself to the fashionable interiors of the period.

While Mackintosh's work is rare and correspondingly costly he did influence other Scottish designers who adapted his style sufficiently to make it acceptable to commercial companies. These included George Logan and Ernest Archibald Taylor who designed for Wylie and Lochhead, and George Walton who had his own firm of interior designers in Glasgow but began to design for Liberty in 1897. Taylor moved to Manchester in 1908 to work for George Wragge Ltd. and, like Logan

Sideboard, mahogany with marquetry
Height: 138.6cm
Furniture Store, London
Price: £900

and Walton, he designed pieces which still retain the characteristics of the Glasgow style but with less emphasis on upward surging line and tapering forms.

Frances and Margaret Macdonald were both involved in the revival of embroidery in Glasgow in the 1890s.

Jessie R. Newbery taught the subject at the Glasgow School of Art and she and her pupils produced a wide range of pieces decorated with abstract and semi-abstract designs which emphasized the shapes of collars, belts and other items. Embroidery was regarded as a serious aspect of design and *Studio* published patterns and organized competitions for embroiderers. The effect of the embroidery revival was twofold: machinemade embroidery produced for the fashion industry began to reflect the designs of the Glasgow School after the turn of the century (many of the embroidered blouses sold by Swan and Edgar for example had delicate designs on their collars and yokes which can be traced back to patterns devised by Margaret Macdonald, Frances Macdonald and Jessie M. King), and crafts guilds that were founded in the second half of the nineteenth century produced embroidered works on every scale from needlepoint intended for upholstery to collars, cuffs and other accessories. The work produced by the anonymous members of the crafts guilds was often extremely skilful and, by the turn of the century, incorporated Art Nouveau motifs from both the Glasgow School and other sources.

Chair, oak with pewter inlay
Height: 94cm
Sold: Phillips, London, 21/10/86
Price: £132

AMERICAN DESIGNS

In America furniture design was predominately revivalist. Art Nouveau made less impact on the furniture market in the States than in Europe, and it was only as late as 1893 that the exhibits in the Chicago World Fair showed an overriding concern with historical styles. French rococo was a particular favourite, and Gothic (the so-called 'Eastlake Style') was also extremely popular. The Arts and Crafts movement had a considerable impact in America, encouraged by visits to that country by Dr Christopher Dresser, Walter Crane and C.R. Ashbee and exhibitions of work by Voysey. Gustav Stickley and Elbert Hubbard (who founded the Roycroft Community) both visited Britain, and their subsequent work shows the influence of Morris and of the Arts and Crafts guilds.

On the whole the British influence

did not lead to any adoption of Art Nouveau; Stickley's own work and that publicized in his magazine *The Craftsman* was simple, well constructed and devoid of any references to the organic elements of Art Nouveau. In California, Henry and Charles Sumner Greene adapted the Japanese influence to produce handmade furniture often inlaid with panels of metals or carving in the Oriental style. The Furniture Shop in San Francisco, founded by Arthur F. Mathews and his wife Lucia, produced a wide range of objects including furniture which were made by a team of craftsmen to their design. Furniture Shop pieces are often inlaid or painted with designs which reflect French Art Nouveau but the overall shapes of the pieces themselves remain fairly conventional.

One of the few American designers to adapt Continental Art Nouveau was Charles Rohlfs whose furniture, always handbuilt and usually commissioned, was perhaps the closest to that style, with its complex rhythms and interlaced lines. On the whole the mass manufacturers of furniture in America were reluctant to accept the new style, but textile companies such as M.H. Birge and the York Wallpaper Company were more willing to experiment, and both produced designs at the turn of the century which show a clear French influence.

FURNITURE AND TEXTILES IN FRANCE

In France, Paris and Nancy were the two cities from which the best Art Nouveau furniture came. In both centres furniture was made as an aspect of interior design. At the 1900 Exhibition in Paris, room settings were shown designed as complete units, and the shops of both Siegfried Bing and Julius Meier-Graefe in Paris consisted of suites of rooms conceived specifically to enhance and complement the furniture that both men commissioned from the designers they patronized.

At his Maison de l'art Nouveau Siegfried Bing sold work by Georges de Feure, Eugène Gaillard and Edward Colonna. De Feure was also

Writing desk, mahogany with marquetry
Height: 128.5cm
Sold: Sotheby's, London, 16/5/86
Price: £880

a graphic designer, and his work for Bing displays the same characteristics as his graphic art; at times he seems to be 'drawing' with the wood, and his chairs and couches are composed of delicate linear patterns which frame panels of textiles, also designed by him. Gaillard's work is more robust, the linear expression used by de Feure replaced by stronger, swirling lines which swell at the base to give stability to the forms of his furniture. Colonna, who also designed jewellery for Bing, used simpler forms with an emphasis on undecorated surfaces framed by elegantly controlled lines.

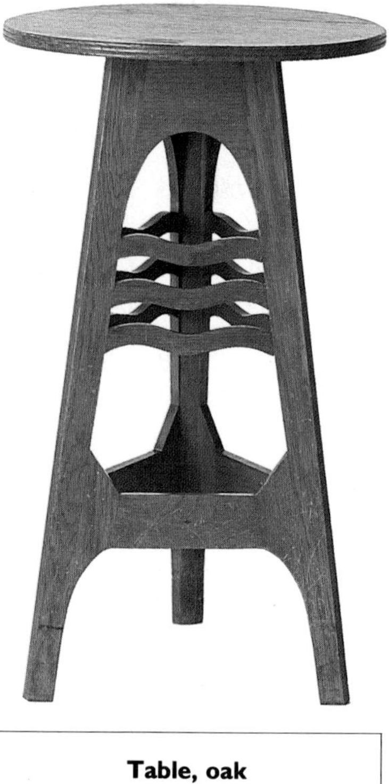

Table, oak
Height: 76.5cm
Furniture Store, London
Price: £90

At La Maison Moderne, Meier-Graefe sold furniture designed by Henry van de Velde, Paul Follot, Maurice Dufrêne and Abel Landry. Van de Velde, Follot and Landry worked in a rhythmic, abstract style; Follot was particularly praised for the abstract simplicity of his work which, as a contemporary critic remarked, 'did not convey the fantasy or nervousness of the age'. Dufrêne's work was also restrained; at the turn of the century he was beginning to abandon curving lines in favour of a more geometric style of abstraction.

Alexandre Charpentier, Charles Plumet and Tony Selmersheim were part of a group which called itself 'Les Six'. Charpentier's work characteristically incorporated wooden carved panels in low relief whereas Plumet and Selmersheim made pieces with strong, organic forms. Another designer, Georges Hœntschel was more naturalistic, often using complex and carefully observed plant forms in his work. Hector Guimard evolved a highly personal form of Art Nouveau in the mid-nineties, designing pieces which seem almost alive. Typically, his designs are asymmetrical with large masses linked by slender, tense lines and with glazed panels expressed as organically curving shapes, often crossed by delicate, sinuous lines.

The most influential designer connected with the furniture-makers in Nancy was Emile Gallé. His own work was directly inspired by nature and he often incorporated marquetry panels into his pieces which depicted stylized landscapes of foliage or flowers against a formalized sky or water. Louis Majorelle was directly influenced by Gallé, translating his naturalism into a more abstract style while still using the exotic and strongly grained woods favoured by him. Majorelle also used gilt bronze to embellish his furniture and to emphasize the junction of one form with another.

The 'Ecole de Nancy, Alliance Provinciale des Industries d'Art' was founded by Gallé in 1901 and included among its members Jacques Gruber, Eugène Vallin and Emile André. Gruber worked for both Majorelle and for the Daum brothers.

GERMAN AND AUSTRIAN DESIGNS

Mass production played an important role in the development of Art Nouveau in both Germany and Austria. In Germany the collaboration between designer and industry was as fruitful as in England and many artists followed the lead of Karl Schmidt and designed specifically with machine production in mind. On the whole their furniture was simple in its forms, which meant that a design could be reproduced successfully without losing any of its quality in the manufacturing process. However, there were some exceptions: Bernhard Pankok, for example, made several designs which were extremely rich and ornate.

Richard Riemerschmid, Karl Bertsch, and Bruno Paul all designed pieces with surfaces devoid of decoration but with tapering lines and inventive juxtapositions of shape. Riemerschmid's long-case clock for example, designed in 1902, has an elongated and tapering body terminating in a rectangular 'head' which houses the clock face. The two forms are linked by supporting rods which visually anchor the elements of the design.

Chair, oak, by Charles Plumet and Tony Selmersheim
Height: 89cm
Sold: Phillips, London, 21/10/86
Price: £374

The Deutscher Werkbund produced a wide range of designs which were constantly modified. Karl Schmidt was responsible for the marketing of their work, a job which he approached in a very professional way. A design was never permitted to remain on the market for more than one year before it was withdrawn and replaced; this applied equally to furniture, carpets and textiles designed by the Werkbund.

In 1899 van de Velde moved to Germany, where he produced some furniture; he was particularly in-

Table, beech and marquetry, by Louis Majorelle
Height: 74.8cm
Sold: Phillips, London, 21/10/86
Price: £572

fluential in the discipline of textile design with his graphic, linear style which emphasized the flat surface and also adapted well to commercial printing techniques. Several German designers were involved in the design of wallpapers, and van de Velde's influence can be seen again in the restrained colours and abstract shapes of the best of them. Art Nouveau furniture was mass-produced in Germany by a number of companies; for instance, Otto Weinhold designed for Mobelfabrik Olbernau in Saxony which manufactured some of the best mass-produced furniture.

The Wiener Werkstätte in Austria was dependent on outside companies to produce designs intended for mass manufacture because the Werkstätte's own workshops executed pieces, including furniture, which

were too costly in their materials or too intricate in their construction for machine production. Initially, however, all the designs produced by the association were manufactured by them. Companies which manufactured for the Werkstätte included Kunstmobelfabrik August Ungethüm; the Werkstätten für Wohnungseinrichtung, M. Niedermoser & Sohne and Portois & Fix, all of which were based in and around Vienna. A number of architects and designers submitted work to the Werkstätte; Otto Wagner, Adolph Loos and Otto Prutscher were among those who contributed designs for furniture.

Desk, teak, by Otto Fritzsche
Height: 73.7cm
Sold: Christie's South Kensington, London, 9/5/86
Price: £702

Werkstätte furniture is characterized by its apparent simplicity, Josef Hoffmann, Kolo Moser and their teacher Otto Wagner all designed pieces which are geometric in their outlines, with no curving or sinuous lines; the influence of Mackintosh was particularly strong in Vienna and is obvious in Hoffmann's use of elongated forms and of lattice work. Hoffmann, Moser and Wagner used costly woods and other rich materials in their work particularly towards the end of the 1900s; this marriage of simple forms with exquisite materials can be seen in Hoffmann's work for the Palais Stoclet in Brussels for which he was both architect and, with Moser, furniture and interior designer. Hoffmann's earlier work is more accessible to the collector; his work and Wagner's was mass produced and some of Hoffmann's designs have been reproduced recently along with those of Mackintosh.

Two Viennese firms manufacturing bentwood furniture, Thonet Brothers and Jacob & Josef Kohn, commissioned designs from Secession artists. Before 1900 Gustave Siegel, one of Josef Hoffmann's students, was appointed as artistic consultant to Kohn. As well as designing for the firm himself, he also commissioned designs from Hoffmann and Otto Wagner. Thonet commissioned designs from Hoffmann, Wagner, Adolf Loos and Kolo Moser.

DESIGN IN BELGIUM

Before moving permanently to Germany, Henry van de Velde had worked in his native Belgium where he evolved his theories of design and developed the style that was influential in Paris as well as in Germany. His furniture was organic in form – van de Velde believed in adapting the principles of growth to achieve a vital and tense line in his work. The room settings made by him for Meier-Graefe exhibit this organic dynamism in the furniture and in the textiles, particularly in the patterns of the large rugs.

Victor Horta was more luxurious in his work than van de Velde; his furniture, most of which was designed for rooms also designed by him, was opulent and full of swirling, complex lines. Both Horta and van de Velde exerted a considerable influence on Belgian designers working in the applied arts in the 1890s. In turn, van de Velde was influenced by Gustave Serrurier-Bovy who opened a factory at Liège in order to mass produce his designs.

Chair, beech
Height: 88cm
Furniture Store, London
Price (set of 5): £290

DUTCH DESIGN

Some of the most exciting and innovative Art Nouveau textiles came from Holland where the Japanese influence was less important in this area of design than the influence of Indonesian textile designs and techniques. The designer and painter Jan Thorn-Prikker adapted the traditional Javanese technique of batik printing to his own two-dimensional patterns which were sold through *t'Binnenhuis*, the arts and crafts shop in The Hague. Michael Duco Crop adapted some of these ideas for machine production in the designs he made for P.F. van Vlissingen and Co. of Helmond. The relevance of Indonesian designs to Art Nouveau in the Netherlands was enhanced by the emphatically rhythmic treatment of their surface patterns. Futhermore, the batik technique, with its inherently organic quality, could easily be adapted to designs which were based on natural forms.

ITALIAN STYLES

Italy produced designers who contributed personal and idiosyncratic interpretations of Art Nouveau. In Italy Carlo Bugatti made furniture which was executed in combinations of carved woods, painted vellum and various metals. After the turn of the century he modified his style which became rather less ornamented and more curvilinear. After 1905 his designs were manufactured by the Milan firm De Vecci. Eugenio Quarti, a friend of Bugatti, also made opulent furniture in a style which was more markedly French than Bugatti's. But he too adopted a more restrained style after the turn of the century and began producing pieces which were often painted white, with simplified floral motifs.

In common with its decline as a style in the other branches of the applied arts, Art Nouveau furniture and textile design suffered from endless and often misinformed reproduction and elaboration. The principles of organic shape and formalization were abused so that, by the end of the first decade of the twentieth century, completely impractical furniture embellished with inappropriate motifs was being mass produced all over Europe. Some of the most innovative designs were already moving towards a more geometric style which became more prevalent during the years preceding the First World War.

Bentwood plant stand, designed by Gustav Siegel for J. & J. Kohn
Height: 130cm
Sold: Sotheby's, New York, 11/10/86
Price: $1100

Object	Quality of manufacture	Quality of design and/or decoration	Rarity	Price (£)	Price ($)
Anon.					
side chair	7	6	■	35–100	56–160
dining chairs (6)	7	6	■■	250–750	400–1200
writing desk, fall front	7	7	■■	700–1000	1120–1600
desk	7	7	■	200–750	320–1200
sideboard	7	7	■	400–800	640–1280
display cabinet	7	7	■	700–1000	1120–1600
occasional table	7	7	■	75–150	120–240
dining table	7	7	■■	200–600	320–1000
pair of curtains	7	7	■■■	400–800	640–1280
table cloth	7	7	■■■	250–500	400–800
portière	7	7	■■■	300–600	480–1000
carpet	7	7	■■■	500–1000	800–1600
Bugatti, C.					
mirror	8	9	■■■	800–1000 +	1280–1600 +
stool	8	9	■■	800–1000 +	1280–1600 +
side chair	8	9	■■	900–1000 +	1440–1600 +
Davenport, A.					
side chair	8	7	■■	200–500	320–800
occasional table	8	7	■■	250–500	400–800
dining table	8	7	■■■	400–800	640–1280
Gallé, E.					
marquetry tray	9	8	■■■	500–1000	800–1600
occasional table	9	8	■■	600–1000 +	1000–1600 +
Kohn, J. & J.					
chair	8	7	■■	100–300	160–480
armchair	8	7	■■	200–400	320–640
plant stand (designed by G. Siegel)	8	9	■■■	600–800	1000–1280

Qualities on a scale 1-10 ■ Rare ■■ Very rare ■■■ Extremely rare

Object	Quality of manufacture	Quality of design and/or decoration	Rarity	Price (£)	Price ($)
Liberty					
dressing table	8	7	■ ■	400–600	640–1000
cupboard	8	7	■ ■	200–500	320–800
Majorelle, L.					
side chair	8	9	■ ■ ■	750–1000 +	1200–1600 +
occasional table	8	9	■ ■	500–1000 +	800–1600 +
etagère	8	9	■ ■ ■	900–1000 +	1440–1600 +
Plumet, C. and Selmersheim, T.					
side chair	8	8	■ ■ ■	350–500	560–800
Serrurier-Bovy, G.					
side chair	8	9	■ ■ ■	750–1000 +	1200–1600 +
occasional table	8	9	■ ■ ■	800–1000 +	1280–1600 +
Thonet Bros.					
chair	7	7	■	75–150	120–240
armchair	7	7	■ ■	100–200	160–320
coat stand	7	7	■ ■	100–250	160–400
rocking chair	7	8	■ ■	750–1000	1200–1600

Qualities on a scale 1-10 ■ Rare ■ ■ Very rare ■ ■ ■ Extremely rare

Bibliography

Amaya, Mario *Art Nouveau* (Studio Vista, London, 1966)

Buffet-Challié, Laurence *Art Nouveau Style* (translated by Geoffrey Williams, Academy Editions, London, 1982)

Champigneulle, Bernard *Art Nouveau* (translated by Benita Eisler, Barron's, New York, 1976)

Duncan, Alastair *Art Nouveau Sculpture* (Academy Editions, London, 1978)

Garner, Philippe *Emile Gallé* (Academy Editions, London, 1976)

Gillon, Edmund V. *Art Nouveau: An Anthology of Design and Illustration* (Dover Publications, New York, 1969)

Haslam, Malcolm *Marks and Monograms of the Modern Movement* (Charles Scribner's Sons, New York, 1977)

Heskett, John *Design in Germany 1870–1918* (Trefoil Books, London, 1986)

Hofstätter, Hans H. *Art Nouveau Prints, Illustrations and Posters* (Omega Books, Ware, 1984)

Howard, Thomas *Charles Rennie Mackintosh and the Modern Movement* (Routledge & Kegan Paul, London, 1952)

Johnson, Diane C. *American Art Nouveau* (Harry N. Abrams, New York 1979)

Kallir, Jane *Viennese Design and the Wiener Werkstätte* (Galerie St Etienne/George Braziller, New York, 1986)

Koch, Robert *Louis C. Tiffany, Rebel in Glass* (Crown Publishers, New York, 1964)

Madsen, Stephan Tschudi *Sources of Art Nouveau* (Da Capo Press, New York, 1976)

Masini, Lara-Vinca *Art Nouveau* (translated by Linda Fairbairn, Thames & Hudson, London, 1984)

Pevsner, Nikolaus *Pioneers of Modern Design* (Penguin Books, Harmondsworth, 1960)

Schmutzler, Robert *Art Nouveau* (translated by Edouard Roditi, Harry N. Abrams, New York, 1962)

Selz, Peter H., and **Constantine,** Mildred *Art Nouveau, Art and Design at the Turn of the Century* (Museum of Modern Art, New York, 1975)

Sterner, Gabriele *Art Nouveau* (translated by Frederick G. Peters and Diana S. Peters, Barron's, New York, 1982)

Waddell, Roberta (ed) *The Art Nouveau Style* (Dover Publications, New York, 1977)

Index

Pages in italics contain illustrations